# WOMEN POETS
# OF THE WEST:
# An Anthology, 1850-1950

Ahsahta Press

Boise State University
Boise, Idaho

# Acknowledgments

**Mary Austin:**
Poems from **The Children Sing in the Far West** by Mary Austin. Copyright 1928 by Mary Austin, Copyright renewed 1956 by Kenneth M. Chapman and Mary C. Wheelright. Reprinted by permission of Houghton Mifflin Company.

Poems from **The American Rhythm**, 2nd edition, by Mary Austin. Copyright 1923 and 1930 by Mary Austin, Copyright renewed 1958 by Kenneth M. Chapman and Mary C. Wheelright. Reprinted by permission of Houghton Mifflin Company.

**Peggy Pond Church:**
Peggy Pond Church for poems from her **New & Selected Poems** (Boise: Ahsahta Press, 1976).

**Alice Corbin:**
Mrs. Edgar L. Rossin for Alice Corbin's poems from **Red Earth, Poems of New Mexico** (Chicago: Ralph Fletcher Seymour, 1920) and **The Sun Turns West** (Santa Fe: Writers' Editions, 1933).

**Peggy Simson Curry:**
Peggy Simson Curry for poems from her **Red Wind of Wyoming**, 3rd edition (Denver: Sage Books, 1955).

**Hildegarde Flanner:**
Hildegarde Flanner for poems from her **Time's Profile** (New York: Macmillan, 1929) and **If There Is Time** (Norfolk, Connecticut: New Directions, 1942).

**Sharlot Hall:**
The Sharlot Hall Historical Society of Arizona, Prescott, Arizona, for Sharlot Hall's poems from **Poems of a Ranch Woman** (Prescott: Sharlot Hall Historical Society, 1953).

**Gwendolen Haste:**
Gwendolen Haste for poems from her **Selected Poems** (Boise: Ahsahta Press, 1976).

**Janet Lewis:**
Janet Lewis for poems from her *Poems, 1924-1944*, Copyright 1950, by permission of The Swallow Press, Inc.

**Genevieve Taggard:**
A poem from *Travelling Standing Still: Poems 1918-1928*, by Genevieve Taggard. Copyright 1928 by Alfred A. Knopf, Inc. and renewed in 1956 by Kenneth Durant. Reprinted by permission of the publisher.

Poems from *Collected Poems, 1918-1938*, by Genevieve Taggard. Copyright, 1938 by Harper & Row, Publishers, Inc. Courtesy of the publisher.

A poem from *Origin: Hawaii, 1947* [Honolulu: Donald Angus], Copyright 1949 by the Estate of Genevieve Taggard. Copyright renewed by Marcia Durant Liles, March, 1975.

In addition to the above-named individuals and firms, the editor would like to make grateful acknowledgment for the service provided by the staff of the Boise State University Inter-Library Loan Department, the courtesies extended by libraries throughout the West, the helpful suggestions and long-distance sleuthings of Miss Josephine Miles, and the welcome assistance of Maureen Ursenbach Beecher with the poems and sketch of Eliza Snow.

Poems selected and edited and biobibliographies composed by
A. Thomas Trusky

Third, Revised Edition
December 1981

ISBN 0-916272-08-7

Library of Congress Catalog Card Number:
77-83227

꞊ift (E.Forther)

# Contents

**Note:**  the poems in this anthology are presented in chronological order, according to the date of their appearance in a volume.

A centered asterisk has been employed to indicate where poems have been broken, mid-stanza. (Asterisked poem titles, however, indicate a note to the poem has been supplied by the author or previous editor.)

# Introduction

This anthology focuses on the west—its landscape, people, and character—and on women in the west going about their lives on ranches, homesteads, in small towns and suburbia, all as seen by western poets. Most of the poets here are participants in the westward movement that has gone on since our country began. Though with two exceptions they are not native to the west, most have assimilated the western landscape and the western openness of feeling, both spatial and psychological, into their poems.

The land into which these writers came stretches from the eastern slopes of the Rockies to the islands of Hawaii in the Pacific, and from the Canadian to the Mexican borders. It is a vast stretch of continent and shoreline embracing the most varied of landscapes, dramatic in its contrasts, from the high peaks of the mountain ranges to plains or deserts through which rivers have cut deep channels and wind has eroded buttes into fantastic contours. For all its variety, perhaps no region demonstrates better than the west the power of the landscape over the writers within it. Not only have the writers in this anthology used landscape, but the landscape has shaped the subject and symbols of its writers. No one can read the poets here without being conscious of the western land as a participant in the lives of its people.

This volume includes poems by women who have lived in various parts of the west, poems written over a period of about a hundred and twenty years. Yet this very largeness of space and time encompasses as well as separates, and we find in these writers certain intersections of design and subject.

In the course of the anthology we see the westering of our people. The poets look on the land and describe it, then they enter it and make themselves homes in it, though the land still dominates. Finally, as in the work of some of the last poets in the book, the land has been subordinated, at least in certain areas. Except for Eliza R. Snow, who was born in Massachusetts, and Peggy Simson Curry, born in Scotland, these newcomers are midwesterners from the tiers of states adjoining the western land, from Illinois, Kansas, Iowa, Minnesota, and farthest east, Indiana.

The first four women were in the truest sense pioneers, coming by wagon train before the transcontinental railroad was completed in 1869. Eliza R. Snow, perhaps the first woman poet of the west, came with the first wave of Mormon immigrants into the valley of the Great Salt Lake in 1847-48. During the journey along the Platte River and across the mountains she wrote hymns, wedding poems, acrostics, and elegies on some of those who died in great numbers along the way. But long before this journey, she had been interested in writing about the new lands. When she left Massachusetts for the mid-west, she wrote in Wordsworthian measures of her first view of the prairie, and she wrote sympathetically of the native Americans when in the 1830s Congress proposed to move the southern Indians to the west. Regarding the plight of the western Indians, she complained, as would many a modern environmentalist, that the white man was about "to fell the last forest, and burn up the wild." But once the new Zion was settled, much of Snow's poetry consisted of hymns for the newly founded religion.

Ella Higginson was another poet known chiefly for her songs. Taken as a child from Kansas to Oregon, she lived most of her life in Bellingham, Washington. Her lyrics evoke nature in fairly general terms and make only occasional references to the dramatic scenery of the northwest, as when she speaks of "Puget Sea" or "the purple West."

Ina Coolbrith, who traveled to Los Angeles in 1851, then moved to San Francisco where she lived until her death in 1928, was the first of these poets to use the west, its landscape, place-names, people, and history, as subject and background of her poems. Much of her early poetry was written during the period when local color was emphasized in fiction, especially in short stories such as those of her associates Bret Harte and Mark Twain. Most of her poems reflect in some way the California scene, though it is a California immersed in romanticism and elaborate rhetoric ("great Shasta," "silvery mission bells") that we have moved away from today.

Sharlot Hall, a generation younger than Ina Coolbrith, looked at the west with a more realistic eye. She was herself a ranch woman and describes more closely what she really sees. She catalogs the desert plants in "Spring in the Desert" and "The Water Tank at Dusk." She writes too of the native Americans, though they do not loom so large in her world as the Mexicans of the villages on both sides of the border. Sharlot Hall, who managed a ranch while serving as associate editor of Charles F. Lummis's magazine **Out West**, spoke in modern terms of the place of woman in such poems as "The Reply of the Free Woman" and the satiric "Man-Sized Job."

The themes of drouth and isolation first expressed by Hall are taken up in even greater detail by Gwendolen Haste in Montana, Peggy Pond Church in New Mexico, and Nellie Burget Miller in Colorado. These poets are especially aware of the loneliness of ranchers, homesteaders, and nomadic shepherds.

Most of the early poets wrote in traditional measures and rhyme, putting the experience of the west into the forms available to them. At times there seemed to be a discrepancy between the old ways of poetry and the materials of the new land. Even as early as Snow, the running rhythms reminiscent of Sir Walter Scott employed in "The Red Man of the West" seem out of place. Sharlot Hall used the ballad rhythms effectively in her narratives of western events, though they are overly emphatic for an otherwise fine descriptive poem like "Spring in the Desert."

Two poets, Mary Austin and Alice Corbin, who had studied the songs of the native Americans, found in them a way of providing a more indigenous rhythm for western poets. Mary Austin set forth the principles of "The American Rhythm" in her famous essay of that name. The American rhythm was to be based on the naturally recurring pulses—those of the heart, those of the footsteps. Mary Austin's discovery of such rhythms coincided with the introduction of so-called "free verse," which also broke away from the metrical tradition. Alice Corbin was the associate editor of **Poetry**, which published much of the new poetry and its manifestos during the years 1915 to 1920 when free verse became popular. She too moved to Santa Fe and, like Austin, translated the songs of the native Americans and carried over the new rhythms into her own original verse.

Important, however, to the emergence of a new kind of poetry after 1920 was the example of the clear images and direct voice of the native poetry. Earlier, the Imagists and their successors. too, worked through the concrete image toward the meaning of the poem, eschewing the elaborate "poetic" rhetoric of their predecessors. The imagistic movement, together with the example of native styles found in Austin and Corbin, changed American poetry, even for those who wrote in traditional meters.

But the lyric clear of romantic effusion and capable of stark description had been available before this time for those still working in formal measures. Genevieve Taggard was writing such poetry as early as 1914, using the lush vegetation of Hawaii as a setting for her early love poems, and Gwendolen Haste was able to evoke the hard life of the Montana homesteaders and their wives in measured stanzas suggesting by their very bounds the restrictions of life under harsh conditions.

Two California poets have used a more modern series of western scenes. Janet Lewis, born in Chicago, lived in Santa Fe from 1923 to 1928, then moved to Los Altos, near Stanford, where she has lived since. Hildegarde Flanner, born in Indiana, lived for many years near Los Angeles and now resides in the Napa Valley of northern California. Both these poets are superb and conscientious craftsmen, often using descriptions of some aspect of the west as subjects of meditation.

The poems in this anthology have in part been chosen to illustrate what their authors had to say about the land to which they came. Except for Snow, Higginson, and Hazel Hall, most of these writers demonstrate in all their writing a firm sense of place, using the history, landscape, and characters of the west as subject or background. Most are comfortable in the western landscape, finding it part of their thoughts and movements.

What these and other western writers have accomplished is to build for the west a set of symbols and understandings, or a series of sets, for the various areas of this broad land.

From the beginning there is a concern for or an interest in the native Americans. We find this in Snow's early poems, in those of Sharlot Hall, in the romantic narratives of Coolbrith, and culminating in the translations from native American songs by Austin and Corbin.

In the poems too are many references to the Mexican inhabitants of the southwest, people who settled the land before the Yankees came. Many of these are shepherds, and the shepherd as a symbol of isolation recurs again and again in the work of such writers as Sharlot Hall, Peggy Pond Church, and Peggy Simson Curry.

Even more frequent is the idea of drouth. Except for the Pacific northwest, drouth is seasonal and cyclic in the west, and in many of these poets drouth becomes a recurring symbol. Drouth represents the hardness of life and spiritual despondency, as in Peggy Pond Church's poem "Drought" and in Haste's description:

> . . . one by one her little hopes had fled
> Down through those racking, windy, drouth-filled years,
> The frozen winter when the cattle died,
> The year the hail bent flat the tender wheat,
> The thirsty summers with their blazing heat—

Rain is the symbol of renewal. As Sharlot Hall put it:

> Then, at last, a cool dawn wind
> Pitying and deeply kind,
> Brings a far-off scent of rain.
> Ah, the sick earth lives again!

In Miller's poem beginning "The sun drops red through a curtain of dust," no rain is on the way; the tumbleweed blows, the plain is alkali, the brown grass lies in the fields, yet for the poet "deep in my heart is the sound of rain." So long as there is hope of rain, the westerner may conquer the desolation of the spirit which is represented repeatedly by drouth.

It is toward these recurring images of a cycle of drouth and spiritual regeneration that the landscape pushes the western poets, if the spirit is capable of being revived at all. For some of the characters in these poems, regeneration comes too late or never, as with the wife in Haste's "Exotic" whose "soul had withered like last year's weeds."

The green watery landscape of Hawaii suggests poems of love and fertility, and this is what landscape evoked in many of Taggard's poems. The narrow ledge of land between the mountains and the Pacific early became urban; there were small cities there in the time of Ina Coolbrith. She and later California poets write from an urban, often cosmopolitan, point of view, for they live in a gentler land.

But the still unconquered land between the Rockies and the Coast

Range brings forth harsher symbols. The most pervasive image, that created most often and most strikingly in these pages, is the figure of the lonely woman in an isolated homestead, watching the road for some meaningful contact with the world.

In the last line of Snow's wholly conventional poem on woman's duty, she has said, "give to woman fortitude." It is loneliness and the fortitude to encounter and endure loneliness that strikes through the work of even the most urban of these poets—the poetic dreams of the lonely seamstress, the Montana wives, the woman in the field, the woman who left the deserted American farm, the woman touching a parched unopening rose, the lonely shepherds, the great empty shell of the dream of the dirigible, the lonely sound of the freight train passing in the night.

Loneliness, space, fortitude, enforced by a stark expansive landscape, are the symbols that permeate this book. It was for the poets to coalesce this feeling, to distill it from the vastly varying regions of the west, for, in the words of Hildegarde Flanner, when

. . . patience like the burning of a rock
Turns passion, then will the land be ours.

Then will the native heart be cleared for use.

In other words, the land will be ours only when the poets have entered and possessed it. In this anthology we see this possessing come to pass.

*Ann Stanford*
Beverly Hills, California
April, 1978

# Eliza R. Snow

# The Red Man of the South *

How long shall we be hunted, like foxes in the chase,
And, like the wild-deer, made to fly before the white man's face?
How long will av'rice govern you, ye haughty sons of pride?
How long will fraud attest your claim, and force, the right decide?

Once we were savage wanderers, wild as our own rude bowers;
We gloried in the wilderness, and thought creation ours;
The forest, our large storehouse, abundant game insur'd,
And, folded in its bosom, we felt ourselves secur'd.

Cast in the mould of nature, our minds an impress took
Congenial with the mountain cliff and the meand'ring brook:
We knew no studied classics: our fathers' feats of old,
Were through tradition's faith preserv'd, and by our mothers told.

You've tam'd our vagrant spirits, and taught us how to prize
The worth of local treasures, the bliss of local joys:
You've taught us manufact'ring skill—we love the tame employ;
You've taught us arts of husbandry—we prize the harvest joy.

You've taught us *home is very dear;* and many a year of toil
Has made *our* homes seem beautiful, here on *our fathers'* soil:
Our souls, of softer texture now, can suit their tastes no more
Among the wild ferocities which satisfied before.

No more the deserts charm us, no more we feel a pride
In ranging o'er the lofty peaks, or by the mountain's side:
Our wants, by knowledge multiplied, would mock our best pretence
To gain, by rude and scanty means, a proper competence.

*The foregoing was written at the time when the subject of removing the Southern Indians to the West was discussed in the Congress of the United States of America, in 1830.

1

Divest us of the habits in civil life acquir'd—
Obliterate the feelings those habits have inspir'd—
Give back our roving natures, our tomahawk and bow—
*Then, with our wives and little ones, to western wilds we'll go.*

# The Red Man of the West

The Great Spirit, 'tis said, to our forefathers gave
All the lands 'twixt the eastern and western big wave;
And the Indian was happy—he'd nothing to fear,
As he rang'd o'er the mountains, in chase of the deer;
And he felt like a prince, as he steer'd the canoe,
Or explor'd the lone wild, with his hatchet and bow—
Quench'd his thirst at the streamlet, or simply he fed,
With the heavens for his curtain, the hillock his bed.
Say, then was he homeless?  No: no, his heart beat
For the dear ones he lov'd, in the wigwam retreat.

But a wreck of the white man came over the wave:
In the chains of the tyrant, he'd learn'd to enslave:
Emerging from bondage and pale with distress,
He fled from oppression—he came to oppress!
Yes, such was the white man, invested with power;
When almost devour'd, he would turn to devour.
He seiz'd our possessions, and, fatt'ning with pride,
He thirsted for glory, but "freedom," he cried.

Our fathers were brave—they contended awhile,
Then left the invader the coveted soil:
The spoiler pursued them, our fathers went on,

*

And their children are now at the low, setting sun:
The white man, yet prouder, would grasp all the shore:
He smuggl'd and purchas'd and coveted more.


    The pamper'd blue Eagle is stretching its crest
Beside the great waters that circle the west;
Behind the west wood, where the Indian retires,
The white man is building his opposite fires,
To fell the last forest, and burn up the wild
Which nature design'd for her wandering child.


    Chas'd into environs, and no where to fly;
Too weak to contend, and unwilling to die!
O, where will a place for the Indian be found?
Shall he take to the skies?   Or retreat underground?


# Invocation, or the Eternal Father and Mother

O my Father, thou that dwellest
   In the high and holy place;
When shall I regain thy presence,
   And again behold thy face?


In thy glorious habitation,
   Did my spirit once reside?
In my first primeval childhood,
   Was I nurtur'd near thy side?


For a wise and glorious purpose,
   Thou hast plac'd me here on earth;
And withheld the recollection
   Of my former friends and birth;

Yet oft-times a secret something
  Whisper'd, "You're a stranger here";
And I felt that I had wander'd
  From a more exalted sphere.


I had learn'd to call thee Father,
  Through thy Spirit from on high;
But, until the Key of Knowledge
  Was restor'd, I knew not why.


In the heavens are parents single?
  No: the thought makes reason stare:
Truth is reason:  truth eternal
  Tells me I've a mother there.


When I leave this frail existence—
  When I lay this mortal by;
Father, Mother, may I meet you
  In your royal court on high?


Then at length, when I've completed
  All you sent me forth to do;
With your mutual approbation,
  Let me come and dwell with you.

# On the Death
# of the Dearly Beloved
# and Much Lamented Father in Israel,
# Joseph Smith, Sen.,

Patriarch over the Church of Jesus Christ of Latter-day Saints,
Who Died at Nauvoo, September 14th, 1840.

Zion's noblest Sons are weeping!
   See her daughters bath'd in tears,
Where the Patriarch is sleeping
   Nature's sleep, the sleep of years!
Hush'd is every note of gladness—
   Every minstrel bows full low,
Every heart is tun'd to sadness,
   Every bosom feels the blow.

Zion's children lov'd him dearly;
   Zion was his daily care:
That his loss is felt sincerely,
   Thousand weeping Saints declare:
Thousands who have shar'd his blessing—
   Thousands whom his service blest,
By his faith and prayers suppressing
   Evils which their lives opprest.

Faith and works divinely blended
   Prov'd his steadfast heart sincere;
And the power of God attended
   His official labors here:
Long he stemm'd the powers of darkness,
   Like an anchor in the flood—
Like an oak amid the tempest,
   Bold and fearlessly he stood.

Years have witness'd his devotions,
  By the love of God inspir'd;
When his spirit's pure emotions
  Were with holy ardor fir'd.
Oft he wept for suff'ring Zion—
  All her sorrows were his own:
When she pass'd through grievous trials,
  Her oppressions weigh'd him down.

Now he's gone—we'd not recall him
  From a paradise of bliss,
Where no evil can befall him,
  To a changing world like this.
His lov'd name will never perish,
  Or his memory crown the dust,
For the Saints of God will cherish
  The remembrance of the just.

Faith's sweet voice of consolation
  Soothes our grief.  His spirit's flown
Upward to a holier station—
  Nearer the celestial throne:
There to plead the cause of Zion
  In the Councils of the just—
In the Court the Saints rely on,
  Pending Causes to adjust.

Though his earthly part is sleeping
  Lowly 'neath the prairie sod,
Soon the grave will yield its keeping—
  Yield to life the man of God:
When the heavens and earth are shaken,
  When all things shall be restor'd,
When the trump of God shall waken
  Those that sleep in Christ the Lord.

# Song of the Desert*

Beneath the cloud-topp'd mountain,
　　Beside the craggy bluff,
Where every dint of nature
　　Is rude and wild enough;
Upon the verdant meadow,
　　Upon the sunburnt plain,
Upon the sandy hillock;
　　We waken music's strain.

Beneath the pine's thick branches,
　　That has for ages stood;
Beneath the humble cedar,
　　And the green cotton-wood;
Beside the broad, smooth river,
　　Beside the flowing spring,
Beside the limpid streamlet;
　　We often sit and sing.

Beneath the sparkling concave,
　　When stars in millions come
To cheer the pilgrim strangers,
　　And bid us feel at home;
Beneath the lovely moonlight,
　　When Cynthia spreads her rays;
In social groups assembled,
　　We join in songs of praise.

Cheer'd by the blaze of firelight,
　　When twilight shadows fall,
And when the darkness gathers
　　Around our spacious hall,
With all the warm emotion
　　To saintly bosoms given,
In strains of pure devotion
　　We praise the God of heaven.


*Bank of Platte River, Aug. 25, 1847

# What Is, and What Is Not for Woman

'Tis not for her to plough the deep,
   And gather pearls from ocean's bed;
Or scale the rugged mountain's steep,
   For laurel wreaths to deck her head.
She gathers pearls of other name
   Than those the ocean's bosom yields—
Fair laurels never known to fame,
   She culls from wisdom's golden fields.

'Tis not for her to face the foe
   Amid the cannon's thund'ring blaze;
Or shudder at the winds that blow
   Tremendous gales in torrid seas.
But there are foes of other form—
   Of other aspect, she should quell;
And whisper music to the storm,
   When seas of passion rudely swell.

'Tis not for her to lead the van—
   To be ensconced in Chair of State,
To legislate 'twixt man and man—
   Nations and laws to regulate.
'Tis hers to fan the sacred fire
   Of manhood's true nobility—
The heart of nations to inspire
   With patriotism and liberty.

'Tis hers, with heav'nly influence
   To wield a mighty power divine—
To shield the path of innocence
   And virtue's sacred worth define.
'Tis hers to cultivate the germs
   Of all the faculties for good,
That constitute the Godlike forms
   Of perfect man and womanhood.

'Tis hers the sunbeam to sustain
  Amid misfortune's chilling breath—
To silence grief—to solace pain—
  To soothe and cheer the bed of death.
His pathway in the battle lies—
  He should not fear the raging flood:
Give man the breast-plate courage plies,
  But give to woman, *fortitude.*

# Acrostic for Anna Geen*

May the spirit of contentment,
  In your bosom ever dwell:
Such as in the hour of trial
  Sweetly whispers, *"all is well."*

As the blooming rose of summer
  Ne'er withdraws its fragrant breath,
Never may your love & friendship
  And your kindness cease till death.

Greatness, goodness, light & wisdom,
  Endless happiness and peace,
Evermore adorn your pathway—
  Never shall your blessings cease.

*Thursday, March 4, 1847.

9

# Ina Coolbrith

## Retrospect

(In Los Angeles)

A breath of balm—of orange bloom!
  By what strange fancy wafted me,
Through the lone starlight of the room?
  And suddenly I seem to see

The long, low vale, with tawny edge
  Of hills, within the sunset glow;
Cool vine-rows through the cactus hedge,
  And fluttering gleams of orchard snow.

Far off, the slender line of white
  Against the blue of ocean's crest;
The slow sun sinking into night,
  A quivering opal in the west.

Somewhere a stream sings, far away;
  Somewhere from out the hidden groves,
And dreamy as the dying day,
  Comes the soft coo of mourning doves.

One moment all the world is peace!
  The years like clouds are rolled away,
And I am on those sunny leas,
  A child, amid the flowers at play.

# With a Wreath of Laurel*

O winds, that ripple the long grass!
  O winds, that kiss the jeweled sea!
Grow still and lingering as you pass
  About this laurel-tree.

Great Shasta knew you in the cloud
  That turbans his white brow; the sweet
Cool rivers; and the woods that bowed
  Before your pinions fleet.

With meadow scents your breath is rife;
  With redwood odors, and with pine:
Now pause and thrill with twofold life
  Each spicy leaf I twine.

The laurel grows upon the hill
  That looks across the western sea.
O wind, within the boughs be still,
  O sun, shine tenderly,

And bird, sing soft about your nest:
  I twine a wreath for other lands—
A grave! nor wife nor child has blest
  With touch of loving hands.

Where eyes are closed, divine and young,
  Dusked in a night no morn may break,
And hushed the poet lips that sung
  The songs none else may wake:

Unfelt the venomed arrow-thrust,
  Unheard the lips that hiss disgrace,
While the sad heart is dust, and dust
  The beautiful, sad face!

*The placing of this wreath on Lord Byron's grave at Hucknall Torkard
started an agitation out of which grew the restoration of the poet's neglected
resting place.

For him I pluck the laurel crown!
It ripened in the western breeze,
Where Sausalito's hills look down
Upon the golden seas;

And sunlight lingering in its leaves
From dawn until the scarce dimmed sky
Changed to the light of stars; and waves
Sang to it constantly.

I weave, and try to weave a tone,
A touch that, somehow, when it lies
Upon his sacred dust, alone,
Beneath the English skies,

The sunshine of the arch it knew,
The calm that swept its native hill,
The love that wreathed its glossy hue,
May breathe around it still!

# An Emblem

I waited for a single flower to blow,
While all about me flowers were running wild:
Gold-hearted kingcups, sunnily that smiled,
And daisies, like fresh-fallen flakes of snow,
And rarest violets, sweet whole colonies
Nestled in shady grasses by the brooks,
That sang, for love of them and their sweet looks,
Delicious melodies.

Now they are perished, all the fragile throng,
That held their sweetness up to me in vain.
Only this single blossom doth remain,
For whose unfolding I have waited long,

•

Thinking, "How rare a bloom these petals clasp!"
    And lo! a sickly, dwarfed, and scentless thing.
    Mocking my love and its close nourishing,
        And withering in my grasp.

O dream! O hope! O promise of long years!
    Art thou a flower that I have nurtured so,
    Missing the every-day sweet joys that grow
By common pathways; moistened with my tears,
Watched through the dreary day and sleepless night,
    And all about thy slender rootlets cast
    My life like water, but to find at last
        A bitterness and blight?

# Copa de Oro

(California Poppy)

Thy satin vesture richer is than looms
    Of Orient weave for raiment of her kings!
    Not dyes of olden Tyre, not precious things
Regathered from the long-forgotten tombs
Of buried empires, not the iris plumes
    That wave upon the tropics' myriad wings,
    Not all proud Sheba's queenly offerings,
Could match the golden marvel of thy blooms.
For thou art nurtured from the treasure-veins
    Of this fair land:  thy golden rootlets sup
        Her sands of gold—of gold thy petals spun.
Her golden glory, thou! on hills and plains,
    Lifting, exultant, every kingly cup
        Brimmed with the golden vintage of the sun.

# San Francisco

April 18, 1906 *

In olden days, a child, I trod thy sands,
  Thy sands unbuilded, rank with brush and briar
And blossom—chased the sea-foam on thy strands,
  Young City of my love and my desire.

I saw thy barren hills against the skies,
  I saw them topped with minaret and spire;
Wall upon wall thy myriad mansions rise,
  Fair City of my love and my desire.

With thee the Orient touched heart and hands,
  The world-wide argosies lay at thy feet;
Queen of the queenliest land of all the lands—
  Our sunset glory, regal, glad and sweet!

I saw thee in thine anguish tortured! prone!
  Rent with the earth-throes, garmented in fire!
Each wound upon thy breast upon my own,
  Sad City of my grief and my desire.

Gray wind-blown ashes, broken, toppling wall
  And ruined hearth—are these thy funeral pyre?
Black desolation covering as a pall—
  Is this the end—my love and my desire?

Nay! strong, undaunted, thoughtless of despair,
  The Will that builded thee shall build again,
And all thy broken promise spring more fair,
  Thou mighty mother of as mighty men.

Thou wilt arise, invincible! supreme!
  The world to voice thy glory never tire;
And song, unborn, shall chant no nobler theme—
  Great City of my faith and my desire.


* Date of the great earthquake and fire which devastated San Francisco.

14

But I will see thee ever as of old!
  Thy wraith of pearl, wall, minaret and spire,
Framed in the mists that veil thy Gate of Gold—
  Lost City of my love and my desire.

# From Russian Hill

Night and the hill to me!
  Silence no sound that jars;
Above, of stars a sea;
  Below, a sea of stars!

Tranced in slumber's sway,
  The city at its feet.
A tang of salty spray
  Blends with the odors sweet

From garden-close and wall,
  Where the madrona stood,
And tangled chaparral,
  In the old solitude.

Here, from the Long Ago,
  Rezanov's sailors sleep;
There, the Presidio;
  Beyond, the plumèd steep;

The waters, mile on mile,
  Foam-fringed with feathery white;
The beaconed fortress isle,
  And Yerba Buena's light.

O hill of Memories!
  Thy scroll so closely writ
With song, that bough and breeze
  And bird should utter it:

Hill of desire and dream,
  Youth's visions manifold,
That still in beauty gleam
  From the sweet days of old!

Ring out thy solemn tone,
  O far-off Mission bell!
I keep the tryst alone
  With one who loved me well.

A voice I may not hear!
  Face that I may not see,
Yet know a Presence near
  To watch the hour with me. . .

How stately and serene
  The moon moves up the sky!
How silverly between
  The shores her footprints lie!

Peace, that no shadow mars!
  Night and the hill to me!
Below, a sea of stars!
  Above, of stars a sea!

# Listening Back

There are no comrade roses at my window,
  No green things in the lane;
Upon the roof no sibilant soft patter—
  The lullaby of rain;
Without is silence, and within is silence,
  Till silence grows a pain.

Within is silence, and without is silence,
  The snow is on the sill,
In snow the window wreath'd instead of roses,
  And snow is very still . . .
*I wonder is it singing in the grasses,*
  *The rain, on Russian Hill?*

# Ella Higginson

# When the Birds Go North Again

Oh, every year hath its winter,
  And every year hath its rain—
But a day is always coming
  When the birds go North again.

When new leaves swell in the forest,
  And grass springs green on the plain,
And the alder's veins turn crimson—
  And the birds go North again.

Oh, every heart hath its sorrow,
  And every heart hath its pain—
But a day is always coming
  When the birds go North again.

'Tis the sweetest thing to remember
  If courage be on the wane,
When the cold dark days are over—
  Why, the birds go North again.

# Moonrise in the Rockies

The trembling train clings to the leaning wall
  Of solid stone; a thousand feet below
Sinks a black gulf; the sky hangs like a pall
  Upon the peaks of everlasting snow.

Then of a sudden springs a rim of light,
  Curved like a silver sickle.  High and higher—
Till the full moon burns on the breast of night
  And a million firs stand tipped with lucent fire.

# Cradle-Song
# of the Fisherman's Wife

Swung in the hollows of the deep,
While silver stars their watches keep,
   Sleep, my seabird, sleep!
Our boat the glistening fishes fill,
Our prow turns homeward—hush, be still,
   Sleep, my seabird, sleep—
      Sleep, sleep.

The wind is springing from out the West,
Nestle thee deeper in mother's breast,
   Rest, my seabird, rest!
There is no sea our boat could whelm,
While thy brave father is at the helm,
   Rest, my seabird, rest—
      Rest, rest.

The foam flies past us, the lightnings gleam,
The waves break over, the fierce winds scream,
   Dream, my seabird, dream!
Dream of the cot where high and low,
Crimson and white, the roses blow,
   Dream, my seabird, dream—
      Dream, dream.

What tho' the tempest is on the deep?
   Sleep, my seabird, sleep!
Be brave as a fisherman's child should be,
Rocked in the hollows of the sea,
   Sleep, my seabird, sleep—
      Sleep, sleep.

# The Lamp in the West

Venus has lit her silver lamp
  Low in the purple West,
Breathing a soft and mellow light
  Upon the sea's full breast;
It is the hour when mead and wood
  In fine seed-pearls are dressed.

Far out, far out the restless bar
  Starts from a troubled sleep,
Where roaring thro' the narrow straits
  The meeting waters leap;
But still that shining pathway leads
  Across the lonely deep.

When I sail out the narrow straits
  Where unknown dangers be,
And cross the troubled, moaning bar
  To the mysterious sea—
Dear God, wilt thou not set a lamp
  Low in the West for me?


# In the Marsh

I know a dim marsh place where tules grow,
  And mosses cling about the water's edge;
  The tremulous borders deepen, sedge on sedge,
And winds steal thro' them, murmurous and slow;
The dogwood's wingèd blossoms bend and glow
  Like falling stars above the luminous pool—
  How soft they are!  How velvetlike and cool!
Here noiseless serpents, sliding, come and go,
Parting the grasses with a flash of gold.
  The folded water lilies lie asleep,
In shallow cradles, to the drowsy croon
Of sensuous bees.  It is the highest noon,
  Yet all so still the frogs with murmurings deep
Make vocal marsh and wood and summer wold.

# October

October walks these beautiful days
    In a pale, pale lavender gown,
Slashed with the russet of dying leaves
    And bordered with silver down.

Her head is bended, her bronzy hair
    Is wind-blown over her eyes,
And the mantle twisted about her brow
    Is woven of rosy dyes.

Her lips are sad with a mute farewell,
    As she looks in the eyes of the year,
As two that love, yet meet to part
    Without a word or a tear.

She carries an acorn rosary,
    And when each bead has been kissed,
She draws her draperies round her,
    And vanishes thro' the mist.

# Sharlot Hall

# Spring in the Desert

Silence, and the heat lights shimmer like a mist of sifted silver
Down across the wide, low washes where the strange sand rivers flow;
Brown and sun-baked, quiet waveless—trailed with bleaching, flood-swept
   boulders;
Rippled into mimic water where the restless whirlwinds go.

On the banks the gray mesquite trees droop their slender, lace-leafed
   branches;
Fill the lonely air with fragrance, as a beauty unconfessed;
Till the wild quail comes at sunset with her timorous, plumed covey,
And the iris-throated pigeon coos above her hidden nest.

Every shrub distills vague sweetness; every poorest leaf has gathered
Some rare breath to tell its gladness in a fitter way than speech;
Here the silken cactus blossoms flaunt their rose and gold and crimson,
And the proud zahuaro lifts its pearl-carved crown from careless reach.

Like to Lilith's hair down-streaming, soft and shining, glorious, golden,
Sways the queenly palo verde, robed and wreathed in golden flowers;
And the spirits of dead lovers might have joy again together
Where the honey-sweet acacia weaves its shadow-fretted bowers.

Velvet-soft and glad and tender goes the night wind down the canons,
Touching lightly every petal, rocking leaf and bud and nest;
Whispering secrets to the black bees dozing in the tall wild lilies,
Till it hails the sudden sunrise trailing down the mountain's crest.

Silence, sunshine, heat lights painting opal-tinted dream and vision
Down across the wide, low washes where the whirlwinds wheel and
   swing—
What of dead hands, sun-dried, bleaching?  What of heat and thirst and
   madness?
Death and life are lost, forgotten, in the wonder of the spring.

# Sheep Herding

*Many years ago a herd of sheep was feeding its way down from the region around the San Francisco peaks by way of the Verde valley to the desert for the winter. The shepherd sickened and died alone with his sheep.*

*For some weeks thereafter a shepherd dog, very wild and thin, came once in a while to a ranch house on Clear Creek and snatched a little food set out by the woman of the ranch and hurried away. At last he was found to be herding the sheep and guarding the dead body of his master. He had taken the sheep in a small circle to feed and water but had always returned to bed them where he could watch his master's body.*

*In the early and more lonely days of sheep herding it was not uncommon to find the solitary herder insane from loneliness, and one poor man in the state asylum long ago would throw himself on the ground and try to eat grass like the sheep. Another counted incessantly, over and over, keeping tally on imaginary sheep.*

A gray, slow-moving, dust-bepowdered wave,
    That on the edges breaks to scattering spray,
'Round which the faithful collies wheel and bark
    To scurry in the laggard feet that stray;
A babel of complaining tongues that make
    The dull air weary with their ceaseless fret;
Brown hills, akin to those of Galilee,
    On which the shepherds watch their charges yet.

The long, hot days; the stark, wind-beaten nights;
    No human presence, human sight or sound;
Grim, silent land of wasted hopes where they
    Who came for gold oft times have madness found:
A bleating horror that fore-gathers speech,
    Freezing the word that from the lips would pass,
And sends the herdsman grovelling with his sheep,
    Face down and beast-like on the trampled grass.

The collies halt—the slow herd sways and reels,
    Huddled in fear above a low ravine,
Where wild with fright a herd unshepherded
    Beats up and down—with something dark between:
          •

A narrow circle that they will not cross;
A thing to stop the maddest in their run—
A guarding dog, too weak to lift his head,
Who licks a still hand shriveled in the sun.

# The Water Tank at Dusk

*This poem was written during a summer visit to Reed's Ranch, just below the old-time mining camp of Harrisburg in the Harqua Hala desert, one of the loveliest spots in all the desert region of Arizona. The water tank, like a little lake, had been dug out of the adobe earth with softly-rounded earthen banks along which the Yerba Mansa, the beloved and beautiful healing water plant brought by Spanish Fathers from South America, grew tall and rank.*

*A huge cottonwood tree, a feathery-leafed tamarisk, with peach and pear and plum trees and climbing grape vines, shaded this pond and made a cool retreat for all us ranch folk, the small camp of Mohave-Apache Indians, passing Mexicans, freighters, and cowmen, as well as dogs, chickens, birds, bees, and gleaming, peacock-colored dragon flies.*

*The water, pumped by a clanking windmill from a shallow well, ran down into boxes for the herds of cattle and horses that long before dawn began coming in in long, trailing bands, across the desert foothills and mesas, to water while it was still cool.*

*Freighters, with big, high-wheeled wagons on which the wooden brake-blocks chugged and warned us of their coming far away along the desert road, drove in gray with dust, horses rimed with sweat like hoar-frost, to water their teams and rest in the shade.*

*At night all the desert animals beat tiny trails through the sage brush and greasewood and cat claw down to the water to drink.*

*The wild bees worked madly all the moonlight nights upon the blossoms of the giant mesquite trees that covered the bottom of the beautiful, bowl-shaped valley, humming all the while with an irritated tone, as if out of patience because there was so much honey that they had to work day and night and then couldn't save it all.*

*The great, clear-cut hills that seemed so brown and burned in the sun of noon turned to marvelous tones of blue and lavender and opal-pinks at sunset, translucent as rare old glass—so that we seemed to look right through them to the desert which we knew lay beyond. The strange effect of the hills creeping closer at dusk is a lovely bit of desert illusion.*

The wild, bare, rock-fanged hills that all day long
Shut in the hand-width valley from the world,
Like wolfish outposts which no foot might pass,
Creep close as friendly dogs with heads on paws,
And drowsy eyes that watch the evening fire.
Their tawny brown melts into mist
Of rose and violet and translucent blue,
With gold dust powdered softly through the air
That swims and shimmers as if all the earth
Were carven jewels bathed in golden light.
In the soft dusk the desert seems to pant,
Only half-rested from the burning day—
Yet stirs a little happily to feel
The night wind, cool and gentle, whispering
In the white-flowered mesquite where wild bees hum
Delirious with honey sweets and fragrances—
And through the leafless thorn whose tortured boughs
Were wreathed, men say, to crown the suffering Christ
On his high cross—(And still each Passion Week
The sorrowing tree wears buds like drops of blood
In memory.)   With swift, soft whirr of wings
The gray doves flutter down beside the pool,
Cooing their love notes sweet as fairy flutes;
And in the grass the fiddler-crickets chirp.

The spotted night hawk saws his raucous note
Like some harsh rasp upon an o'er-drawn string;
The squeaking bats drop from the cottonwood trees,
Dipping and diving round the shining pool
Where night moths hover like moon-elves astray.
It seems the deep blue sky has fallen there
In the blue, star-set water, where the wind
Makes mimic waves that hardly over-toss
The peach-leaf boat on which the dragon-fly
Rides sailor-wise to rest his gorgeous wings.
The hot, dry, day-time scent of sun-burned sand
Is drowned in sweetness of the blossoming grape,
And pungent odor of the wax-white cups
Of yerba mansa, hedging the blue pool
With a green wall whose every flower
Blooms twice—once on its tall-leafed stalk, and once

*

Down where the waves like silver mirrors mix
Its whiteness with the red pomegranate stars.
In the shadow of the plume-branched tamarisk
There is a half-hushed, honey-throated call,
And from the cottonwood's topmost moonlit bough
Music's enraptured soul seems waked to answer,
So sweet, so low, so pure, so tender-clear;
So brimmed with joy; so wistful, plaintive-sad;
As if all love o' the world pulsed in that throat—
As if all pain o' life beat in the heart below.
It is the mocking bird to his brown mate—
The desert's vesper song of rest and peace.

# The Occultation of Venus

*In March, 1899, I saw the occultation of Venus and the moon from the high hill behind the old mining camp of Congress. It was about three o'clock in the morning when we climbed the hill to wait, wrapped in Indian blankets, for the wind was cold down off the northern ranges.*

*The sky was an inky blue, with stars like needle points; the desert below was a sea of black shadow, with a few lights in the town where others were getting up to see the star and moon meet. The beat of the huge stamps in the mill shook the air and seemed to make the stars quiver and twinkle.*

*Down in the cañon a camp of Mohave-Apache Indians crooned and sang as they waited—for someone had told them that the moon would eat the big white star. When star and moon touched and the star disappeared they began wailing their wild death songs and, when after what seemed a long time the star shone out on the other side of the moon, they shouted and fired their guns in rejoicing.*

A jeweled crown for an old man's brow,
That mystical, splendid blue-dark sky
Arched low o'er the desert, reaching far
Its weary leagues wind-parched and dry.
So bare and lone and sad it lay,
The gray old land that seemed to yearn
With a human longing for tenderness
From its granite barriers grim and stern.

Shouldering up to the very stars
The strong peaks lifted their solemn might;
And through their rock-gapped pinnacles burned
The wondrous glory that charmed the night.
Like a giant's scimitar wrought in gold
The late moon rose in the dawn-touched east,
And close beside white Venus shone,
As once she shone on shrine and priest.

Like a soul's white flame the planet passed—
Alone the moon rode proud and high—
O wait of God!   The lost star swung
A silver sphere in the hither sky—
(Is it so, O Life, that thy light is lost
In the disk of Death if we could but know?)
Then the old land bloomed with a sudden youth
In the tender fire of the morning glow.

# Smell of Rain

Smell of drought on every side;
Every whirlwind flings aside
Acrid, evil-smelling dust
Like some burning mold or musk.
Wind across the garden brings
Scent of blistered, dying things.
Deep corral dust trampled fine
Stings the lips like bitter wine.
Warping boards ooze drops of pitch
Scented with a memory rich
Of cool forests far away.
In the sunbaked fields the hay
Yields a piteous, panting breath
As it slowly burns to death.
Roses in the ranch-house yard
Turn to mummies dry and hard.
Out of dusk and out of dawn
Every fragrance is withdrawn.
Hot, hot winds, and clear, hot sky

Burn the throat and sear the eye.
Then, at last, a cool dawn wind
Pitying and deeply kind,
Brings a far-off scent of rain.
Ah, the sick earth lives again!
Herds that straggle dusty-pale
Down the deep-worn water trail,
Lift their sunken eyes with hope
To the distant mountain slope.
Lean work horses shy and snort
In an awkward, eager sport;
And the ranch dogs, baying, run
Out to meet the rising sun.
In the yard a woman stands,
Touching with bewildered hands
Wan buds trying to unclose
On a parched and dying rose.

# Man-Sized Job

"Wimmin's bizness, it's to cook,
Keep th' house a-goin',
See th' pigs an' chickens fed,
Do a little hoein'
In th' garden summer times,
Jist to keep things growin'!
Cow-men don't like garden dirt
On their han's an' faces.
You won't find no garden truck
'Round real cow-men's places.
That's a job fer wimmin folks,
Like milkin', churnin' butter.
Cow-men never milks no cows.
Hain't no time ter putter.
Keeps me humpin' ridin' range,
Brandin', ropin', tyin';
Runnin' the' whole outfit right—
Wimmins got no use tryin'.
Couldn't run this ranch like me—
Sure, ye couldn't, Maw.
This job calls fer intellec.' . . ."
　　　(Chaw — spit — chaw).

# Pumpkin Pie

*(First Catch Your Pumpkin)*

Select a small pumpkin that's solid and sound.
The large ones are apt to be stringy, I've found.
Peel and cut in small pieces and put in a pot.
Pour over it a quart of water that's hot.
Let it cook for three hours.   Stir once in awhile.
It's best to just simmer, not furiously "bile."
Mash up smooth and fine, and add sugar to taste
And a good lump of butter'll not be a waste.
Clove, nutmeg and ginger, of each one teaspoon,
Of cinnamon, double; and your "sass is now doon."
Stir it well and let simmer.
                                    Meanwhile, you may make
Your crust up, and line the pans ready to bake.
Break six eggs in a dish and beat them up light,
Just whisk all together the yolk and the white.
Add a quart of sweet milk, then two teacups of "sass"
(Or more, if it's needed to form a thick mass).
Pour it into your pans and thoroughly bake.
And if "John" doesn't prefer it to angel's food cake
No woman will be more astonished than I,
For this is *the rule for a prize pumpkin pie!*


# Reply of the Free Woman

The moon is on the little trail that
                    wanders from my door
Among the tall alfalfa blooms all
                    lavender and blue—
And by the wild white clematis as fair as
                    pale star dust
You stand tonight to plead again and vow
                    you will be true.
And I am laughing as you plead, and
                    laughing as you vow—
For if there's need to vow and plead
                    'Twere little use to trust.

# Alice Corbin

## Red Earth

El Rito de Santa Fe

This valley is not ours, nor these mountains,
Nor the names we give them—they belong,
They, and this sweep of sun-washed air,
Desert and hill and crumbling earth,
To those who have lain here long years
And felt the soak of the sun
Through the red sand and crumbling rock,
Till even their bones were part of the sun-steeped valley;
How many years we know not, nor what names
They gave to antelope, wolf, or bison,
To prairie dog or coyote,
To this hill where we stand,
Or the moon over your shoulder . . . .

Let us build a monument to Time
That knows all, sees all, and contains all,
To whom these bones in the valley are even as we are:
Even Time's monument would crumble
Before the face of Time,
And be as these white bones
Washed clean and bare by the sun . . . .

## Corn-Grinding Song

Tesuque Pueblo*

This way from the north
Comes the cloud,
Very blue,
And inside the cloud is the blue corn.

*This song was given me by Canuto Suaza, a Tesuque Indian, who translated it for me from the Tewa, in both Spanish and English. My rendering is as direct as possible.

*How beautiful the cloud*
*Bringing corn of blue color!*

This way from the west
Comes the cloud,
Very yellow,
And inside the cloud is the yellow corn.

*How beautiful the cloud*
*Bringing corn of yellow color!*

This way from the south
Comes the cloud,
Very red,
And inside the cloud is the red corn.

*How beautiful the cloud*
*Bringing corn of red color!*

This way from the east
Comes the cloud,
Very white,
And inside the cloud is the white corn.

*How beautiful the cloud*
*Bringing corn of white color!*

How beautiful the clouds
From the north and the west,
From the south and the east,
Bringing corn of all colors!

# From the Stone Age

Long ago some one carved me in the semblance of a god.
I have forgot now what god I was meant to represent.
I have no consciousness now but of stone, sunlight, and rain;
The sun baking my skin of stone, the wind lifting my hair:
The sun's light is hot upon me,
The moon's light is cool,
Casting a silver-laced pattern of light and dark
Over the planes of my body:
My thoughts now are the thoughts of a stone,
My substance now is the substance of life itself;
I have sunk deep into life as one sinks into sleep;
Life is above me, below me, around me,
Moving through my pores of stone—
It does not matter how small the space you pack life in,
That space is as big as the universe—
Space, volume, and the overtone of volume
Move through me like chords of music,
Like the taste of happiness in the throat,
Which you fear to lose, though it may choke you—
(In the cities this is not known,
For space there is emptiness,
And time a torment) . . . .
Since I became a stone
I have no need to remember anything—
Everything is remembered for me;
I live and I think and I dream as a stone,
In the warm sunlight, in the grey rain;
All my surfaces are touched to softness
By the light fingers of the wind,
The slow dripping of rain:
My body retains only faintly the image
It was meant to represent,
I am more beautiful and less rigid,
I am a part of space,
Time has entered into me,
Life has passed through me—
What matter the name of the god I was meant to represent?

# Cundiyo

As I came down from Cundiyo,
Upon the road to Chimayo
  I met three women walking;
Each held a sorrow to her breast,
And one of them a small cross pressed—
  Three black-shawled women walking.

"Now why is it that you must go
Up the long road to Cundiyo?"
  The old one did the talking:
"I go to bless a dying son."
"And I a sweetheart never won."
  Three women slowly walking.

The third one opened wide her shawl
And showed a new-born baby small
  That slept without a sorrow:
"And I, in haste that we be wed—
Too late, too late, if he be dead!
  The Padre comes tomorrow."

As I went up to Cundiyo,
In the grey dawn from Chimayo,
  I met three women walking;
And over paths of sand and rocks
Were men who carried a long box—
  Beside three women walking.

# On the Acequia Madre

Death has come to visit us today;
He is such a distinguished visitor
Everyone is overcome by his presence—
"Will you not sit down—take a chair?"

But Death stands in the doorway, waiting to depart;
He lingers like a breath in the curtains.
The whole neighborhood comes to do him honor,

*

Women in black shawls and men in black sombreros
Sitting motionless against white-washed walls;
And the old man with the grey stubby beard
To whom death came,
Is stunned into silence.
Death is such a distinguished visitor,
Making even old flesh important.

But who now, I wonder, will take the old horse to pasture?

# Una Anciana Mexicana

I've seen her pass with eyes upon the road—
An old bent woman in a bronze black shawl,
With skin as dried and wrinkled as a mummy's,
As brown as a cigar-box, and her voice
Like the low vibrant strings of a guitar.
And I have fancied from the girls about
What she was at their age, what they will be
When they are old as she.   But now she sits
And smokes away each night till dawn comes round,
Thinking, beside the piñons' flame, of days
Long past and gone, when she was young—content
To be no longer young, her epic done:

> For a woman has work and much to do,
> And it's good at the last to know it's through,
> And still have time to sit alone,
> To have some time you can call your own.
> It's good at the last to know your mind
> And travel the paths that you traveled blind,
> To see each turn and even make
> Trips in the byways you did not take—
> But that, *por Dios*, is over and done,
> It's pleasanter now in the way we've come;
> It's good to smoke and none to say
> What's to be done on the coming day,
> No mouths to feed or coat to mend,
> And none to call till the last long end.
> Though one have sons and friends of one's own.

*

It's better at last to live alone.
For a man must think of food to buy,
And a woman's thoughts may be wild and high;
But when she is young she must curb her pride,
And her heart is tamed for the child at her side.
But when she is old her thoughts may go
Wherever they will, and none to know.
And night is the time to think and dream,
And not to get up with the dawn's first gleam;
Night is the time to laugh or weep,
And when dawn comes it is time to sleep . . . .

When it's all over and there's none to care,
I mean to be like her and take my share
Of comfort when the long day's done,
And smoke away the nights, and see the sun
Far off, a shrivelled orange in a sky gone black,
Through eyes that open inward and look back.


# Walls

A room is four walls—
Made of mud, hide, or bark,
It surrounds and encloses us
Like another skin.

A room is full of a person,
A bodiless form;
Or of several forms
Striving together.

When a house is burned
It is not only
Books, tables, and chairs
That go leaping into the darkness!

I should like to live out of doors,
And let all these images of myself,
Instead of waiting tortured and reproachful,
Go floating off into thin air.

# No Spring

There is no need of any spring to come,
Now autumn holds the burden of my heart,
The sound of robins and of plowmen sowing
Falls like a stone into a pool apart.

For this all springs have come and gone again,
And come once more—to bring this arid taste
Of nothingness and dust; no brown spring flood
Can lift a seed to blossom from this waste.

On days when winter laces naked boughs
Against a riven sky, and the hard earth
Is sealed and frozen, then I do not mind,
For there is nothing to suggest re-birth.

But no one knows how spring may hurt the heart,
Save one who in the spring may have no part.

# Blue Day

The blue day has come back to me.  Somewhere
In mid-most me the day again surges back
And every minutest particle is fair
And I again have my feet on the track
I knew as a child . . . how long I was lost,
How far I had travelled, before this blue gate
Opened again, with no time for the cost,
No need now to hurry, no need now to wait!

Somehow it seems as if I always knew
The day would return again, with deeper blue,
Beckoning inward . . . somehow this day
Motions to something I feared I would miss,
Now gained and recaptured—the ultimate clay
Melting with clay in an ultimate kiss.

# Hazel Hall

## Stitches

Over and under,
Under and out.
Thread that is fibre,
Thread that is stout.

I'm not singing;
I'm sewing.

Days that are futile,
Days that are wise,
Holding the visions
Of dead men's eyes.

I tell you I'm not singing;
If you hear anything
It's my needle.

Days that are prophets
With prophecies
Blunted and tangled
As Eternity's.

I say if you hear anything—

Life-threaded hours;
Purpose that wraps
Fine stitch on fine stitch—
Then ravels. . . and snaps.

## Mending

Here are old things:
Fraying edges,
Ravelling threads;

*

And here are scraps of new goods,
Needles and thread,
An expectant thimble,
A pair of silver-toothed scissors.

Thimble on a finger,
New thread through an eye;
Needle, do not linger,
Hurry as you ply.
If you ever would be through
Hurry, scurry, fly!

Here are patches,
Felled edges,
Darned threads,
Strengthening old utility,
Pending the coming of the new.

Yes, I have been mending. . .
But also,
I have been enacting
A little travesty on life.

# Bead Work

Restless needle, where my beads
Whip with color, roll like seeds,
Dive, and pick up one and one,
One and one till we are done;
And fasten each one firm and true
Where the pattern tells you to—
One and one, and one and one.

One and one, and one and one—
Flying needle, as you run,
As you pick up the lobes of light
Mind you guide each sparkle right;
Mind this tawny brown you choose,
Shading it with light wood hues,

*

When you shape the curving rim
Of this great basket, on whose brim
Heap the designated green,
From new-leaf shades to laurel's sheen.
Then with dawn-pinks and heavy reds
Paint the drowsy roses' heads.
Let dreamy mauves and tones of brass,
And bits of blue in mosaic mass,
Speak for the tints of timid bloom
Which share the shadows' checkered gloom. . .

Sleepy flowers,
Speeding hours,
Hours, flowers, hours. . . .


# Seams

I was sewing a seam one day—
Just this way—
Flashing four silver stitches there
With thread, like this, fine as a hair,
And then four here, and there again,
When
The seam I sewed dropped out of sight. . .
I saw the sea come rustling in,
Big and grey, windy and bright. . .
Then my thread that was as thin
As hair, tangled up like smoke
And broke.
I threaded up my needle, then—
Four here, four there, and here again.

# Lingerie

To-day my hands have been flattered
With the cool-finger touch of thin linen,
And I have unwound
Yards of soft, folded nainsook
From a stiff bolt.
Also I have held a piece of lawn
While it marbled with light
In a sudden quiver of sun.

So to-night I know of the delicate pleasure
Of white-handed women
Who like to touch smooth linen handkerchiefs,
And of the baby's tactual surprise
In closing its fist
Over a handful of nainsook,
And even something of the secret pride of the girl
As the folds of her fine lawn nightgown
Breathe against her body.

# A Baby's Dress

It is made of finest linen—
Sheer as wasp-wings;
It is made with a flowing panel
Down the front,
All overrun with fagot-stitched bow-knots
Holding hours and hours
Of fairy-white forget-me-nots.

And it is finished.
To-night, crisp with new pressing,
It lies stiffly in its pasteboard box,
Smothered in folds of tissue paper
Which envelop it like a shroud—
In its coffin-shaped pasteboard box.

To-morrow a baby will wear it at a christening;
To-morrow the dead-white of its linen
Will glow with the tint of baby skin;
And out of its filmy mystery
There will reach
Baby hands. . . .

But to-night the lamplight plays over it and finds it cold.
Like the flower-husk of a little soul,
Which, new-lived, has fluttered to its destiny,
It lies in its coffin-shaped pasteboard box.

To-morrow will make it what hands cannot;
Limp and warm with babyness,
A hallowed thing,
A baby's dress.

# Instruction

My hands that guide a needle
In their turn are led
Relentlessly and deftly
As a needle leads a thread.

Other hands are teaching
My needle; when I sew
I feel the cool, thin fingers
Of hands I do not know.

They urge my needle onward,
They smooth my seams, until
The worry of my stitches
Smothers in their skill.

All the tired women,
Who sewed their lives away,
Speak in my deft fingers
As I sew to-day.

# The Listening Macaws

Many sewing days ago
I cross-stitched on a black satin bag
Two listening macaws.

They were perched on a stiff branch
With every stitch of their green tails,
Their blue wings, yellow breasts and sharply turned heads,
Alert and listening.

Now sometimes on the edge of relaxation
My thought is caught back,
Like gathers along a gathering thread,
To the listening macaws;
And I am amazed at the futile energy
That has kept them,
Alert to the last stitch,
Listening into their black satin night.

# Late Sewing

There is nothing new in what is said
By either a needle or a thread:
*Stitch*, says a needle, *Stitch*, says the thread;
*Stitch for the living; stitch for the dead;*
*All seams measure the same.*

*Garb for the living is light and gay.*
*While that for the dead is a shrouding grey,*
*But all things match on a later day*
*When little worm-stitches in the clay*
*Finish all seams the same.*

# Mary Austin

## At Carmel

There are people go to Carmel
To see the blue bay pass
Through green wave to white foam
Like snow on new grass.
But I go to hear the auklets crying
Like dark glass on glass.

I go to hear the herons talk
The way that herons have, half asleep,
As they come in past Carmel bar
With a slow wing sleep;
To hear the wood teams jingling up from Sur,
And the contented blether of the Mission sheep.

## The Sandhill Crane

Whenever the days are cool and clear
The sandhill crane goes walking
Across the field by the flashing weir
Slowly, solemnly stalking.
The little frogs in the tules hear
And jump for their lives when he comes near,
The minnows scuttle away in fear,
When the sandhill crane goes walking.

The field folk know if he comes that way,
Slowly, solemnly stalking,
There is danger and death in the least delay
When the sandhill crane goes walking.
The chipmunks stop in the midst of their play,
The gophers hide in their holes away
And hush, oh, hush! the field mice say,
When the sandhill crane goes walking.

# Song of a Youth Whose Father Was Killed in the War*

Something red my father wears now
Where his life was,
Oh, young men, whose wound stripes
    are on your sleeves,
Walk you reverently
Pronouncing my father's name.

Oh, my father,
The old men
Remember you!
I hear them saying
There goes a warrior's son!


*From the Sioux.


# Song of a Man About to Die in a Strange Land*

If I die here
In a strange land,
If I die
In a land I do not know,
Nevertheless, the thunder,
The rolling thunder will take me home.

If I die here, the wind,
The wind rushing over the prairie,
The wind will take me home.


*This is a Chippewa song, which was sung to encourage a good spirit in the young. The Chippewas are the same as the Ojibways, and once lived about the Great Lakes. They are now much scattered, some of them being in Kansas and the Southwest.

The wind and the thunder
They are the same everywhere.
What does it matter then,
If I die here in a strange land.


# Corn-Planting Songs*

(Sung by Osage women as they press the corn seed into the
ground with their feet)

I

Footprints I have made,
Sacred footprints,
Over the corn hill.
Footprints I have made,
They lie in even lines
Firming the planted seed.

Footprints I have made,
Mysterious footprints,
They are broken now
By the small green spears,
Footprints through which come up
Green leafy stalks of the corn.
They wave to each other in the wind.
Footprints I have made,
Over them the young corn ears
Lean to each other in profusion,
Over the footprints I have made
I pluck the foodful ears,
The ripe corn I gather.


*These are Osage songs first collected by Francis La Flesche, an Omaha
Indian who works for the Smithsonian Institution.

44

## II

My footprints, that lie in even lines,
Over them I break the dry stalks,
Gray litter of stalks covers the ground,
From my house gray smoke arises,
There is joy in my house
Because of the abundant corn.

My footprints!
The footprints I have made
They are sacred and mysterious,
Through them life has come,
Life of the corn which is my life,
Through my footprints!

## III

The footprints I have made,
I shall go to see them!
The footprints that lie in even rows.
I shall go to see
The earth broken through the footprints,
The stalks that stand with spreading blades,
The broad blades waving in the wind
I shall go to see.

I shall go to see
The ears that overhang and cross each other,
The ripe ears I shall gather.
I shall go to see
The pale broken ends of stalks
Like blossoms over the field,
I shall go to see the ripened ears
That cause smoke to rise in my house,
That bring joy to my house
The joy of fruition,
The day of harvest!

# Song for the Passing of a Beautiful Woman*

Strong sun across the sod can make
Such quickening as your countenance!

I am more worth for what your passing wakes,
Great races in my loins, to you that cry.
My blood is redder for your loveliness.


*From the Paiute.

# Song of a Woman Abandoned by the Tribe Because She Is Too Old to Keep Up with Their Migration*

Alas, that I should die,
That I should die now,
I who know so much!

It will miss me,
The twirling fire stick;
The fire coal between the hearth stones,
It will miss me.

The Medicine songs,
The songs of magic healing;
The medicine herbs by the water borders,

&ast;

*Southern Shoshone. Among tribes that have no fixed places of residence, the abandoning of old people, too feeble to travel, is usual. This is the only suggestion of protest that I have encountered; the plaint of the aged of all lands that death should ensue just when wisdom is attained. Miss Dinsmore records a similar woman song among the Pima.

They will miss me;
The basket willow,
It will miss me;
All the wisdom of women,
It will miss me.

Alas, that I should die,
Who know so much.

# Genevieve Taggard

## The Enamel Girl

Fearful of beauty, I always went
Timidly indifferent:

Dainty, hesitant, taking in
Just what was tiniest and thin;

Careful not to care
For burning beauty in blue air;

Wanting what my hand could touch—
That not too much;

Looking not to left nor right
On a honey-silent night;

Fond of arts and trinkets, if
Imperishable and stiff

They never played me false, nor fell
Into fine dust.   They lasted well.

They lasted till you came, and then
When you went, sufficed again.

But for you, they had been quite
All I needed for my sight.

You faded, I never knew
How to unfold as flowers do,

Or how to nourish anything
To make it grow.   I wound a wing

With one caress, with one kiss
Break most fragile ecstasies. . . .

Now terror touches me when I
Seem to be touching a butterfly.

# Thirst

There is a bird that hangs head-down and cries
Between the mango leaves and passion vines.
Below a spotted serpent twines
And blunts its head against the yellowing skies.
Along the warping ground a turtle scrapes
And tortured lie glazed fishes in marsh grass.
Across a sky that burnishes like brass
A bat veers stupid with the yeast of grapes.

# With Child

Now I am slow and placid, fond of sun,
Like a sleek beast, or a worn one,
No slim and languid girl—not glad
With the windy trip I once had,
But velvet-footed, musing of my own,
Torpid, mellow, stupid as a stone.

You cleft me with your beauty's pulse, and now
Your pulse has taken body.   Care not how
The old grace goes, how heavy I am grown,
Big with this loneliness, how you alone
Ponder our love.   Touch my feet and feel
How earth tingles, teeming at my heel!
Earth's urge, not mine,—my little death, not hers;
And the pure beauty yearns and stirs.


It does not heed our ecstasies, it turns
With secrets of its own, its own concerns,
Toward a windy world of its own, toward stark
And solitary places.   In the dark
Defiant even now, it tugs and moans
To be untangled from these mother's bones.

# To a Magnificent Spinner, Murdered

Gnats and an ant have gnawed your nimble bones—
You who could spring and sprawl on your own thread
Down half the meadow.   Under tiny stones
The ant has stored your essence.   You are dead.

You stitched the air with level darts; the sun
Slid on your silvers.   Now they slant oblique
Like strokes of rain. . . .
                                        Your neighbors have begun
To chew the cud of festoons.   From the cheek
Of this your hairy enemy dangles one
Loop of his glee to tease your skeleton.

Wasps sting the grapes still, carry spider-spoil
In twisted torment past your web and on
Where their crude honey hangs in muddy cones.
The ants are hurried.   One huge bee intones.
The pond is wrinkled with a velvet oil
Where gnats will hatch, with dusk, another spawn.

# American Farm, 1934

Space is too full.   Did nothing happen here?
Skin of poor life cast off.   These pods and shards
Rattle in the old house, rock with the old rocker,
Tick with the old clock, clutter the mantel.
Waste of disregarded trifles crooked as old crochet
On tabourets of wicker.   Mute boredom of hoarding
Poor objects.   These outlive water sluicing in cracks to join
The destroying river, the large Mississippi; or the tornado
Twisting dishes and beds and bird-cages into droppings of cloud.
The hard odd thing surviving precariously, once of some value
Brought home bright from the store in manila paper,
Now under the foot of the cow, caught in a crevice.
One old shoe, feminine, rotted with damp, one worn tire,
Crop of tin cans, torn harness, nails, links of a chain—
Edge of a dress, wrappings of contraceptives, trinkets,
Fans spread, sick pink, and a skillet full of mould,
Bottles in cobwebs, butter-nuts—and the copperheads,

*

50

Night-feeders, who run their evil bellies in and out
Weaving a fabric of limbo for the devil of limbo;
Droppings of swallows, baked mud of wasps, confetti
Of the mouse nest, ancient cow-dung frozen,
Jumble of items, lost from use, with rusty tools,
Calendars, apple-cores, white sick grasses, gear from the stables,
Skull of a cow in the mud, with the stem of dead cabbage,
Part of the spine and the ribs, in the rot of swill mud.   This
Array of limbo, once a part of swart labor, rusted now,
In every house, in every attic piled.   Oh palsied people!
Under the weeds of the outhouse something one never
Picks up or burns; flung away.   Let it lie; let it bleach.
Ironic and sinister junk filling a corner.   If men vacate,
Prized or unprized, it jests with neglect.
Under the porch the kitten goes and returns,
Masked with small dirt.   Odd objects in sheds and shelves,
And the stale air of bed-rooms, stink of stained bureaus,
Flies buzzing in bottles: vocal tone of no meaning.
No wonder our farms are dark and our dreams take these shapes.
Thistles mock all, growing out of rubbish
In a heap of broken glass with last year's soot.
Implacable divine rubbish prevails.   Possessors of things
Look at the junk heap for an hour.   Gnarled idle hands
Find ticks in the pelt of the dog, turn over a plank.
This parasite clutter invades sense and seems to breed
A like in our minds.   Wind, water, sun;—it survives.
The whole sad place scales to the thistle and petty litter.
Neglect laughs in the fallen barns and the shutters broken
Hanging on a wailing hinge.   Generations of wind
Owe you obeisance.   You win.   No man will war with you.
He has you in him; his hand trembles; he rights
The front acre while the wife tidies the parlour.
Economy, economy!   Who'll till this land?

# The Luau

Odor of algaroba, lure of release.
The smell of red lehua and the crisp scent of maile . . .
These words and images will help you after a little.
Hypnotic words emerge and bloom in the mind,
Anaesthetic names . . . . Dry buzz of bees
Who make a honey eaten at early breakfast
From a comb like a broken coral . . . .
Do dreams foretell the honey?   Break the spell.

So I come home in the valley of Kalihi,
My bare feet on hard earth, hibiscus with stamen-tongue
Twirled in my fingers like a paper wind-mill,
A wheel of color, crimson, the petals large,
Kiss of the petal, tactile, light, intense . . . .

Now I am back again.   I can touch the children:
My human race, in whom was a human dwelling,
Whose names are all the races—of one skin.
For so our games ran tacit, without blur.

What brings me back with giant steps to them?
What was the feast that woke this fabulous thirst?
What was the summer fruit we found and ate
Boldly, with the children of Adam?

A game and a daily search
In the harvest of trees.   We played a parable.
We possessed a valley, devoured the juicy, dense
Jewels of appetite hung in fresco sweeps,
In garlands and in fountains toward the sea.

Mangoes of golden flesh, with turpentine
Peel and odor.   Cut plums of inky stain
And the pucker of persimmons.   Dates to be got
By stepping up a tree-trunk.   Coconuts
With custard centres.   Rose and custard apple,
Eugenia, pink, lemon and little orange,

Guava seedy and tart, and the hidden poha,
And the sacklike fig, to be ripped, to be seen, to be tasted.
How rasping sweet the suck of sugar-cane—
Papaya and banana taken for granted.

With giant steps, in sleep and troubled pain
I return to the fabulous feast, the old communion,
With bodiless hunger and thirst.  Why have I come
Away from the adult world where race is war?

Here we are dipping and passing the calabash
In the ceremony of friends; I also;
But in frenzy and pain distort
The simple need, knowing how blood is shed:
                              *To sit together*
*Drinking the blue ocean, eating the sun*
*Like a fruit . . . .*

# Hildegarde Flanner

## Moment

I saw a young deer standing
Among the languid ferns.
Suddenly he ran—
And his going was absolute,
Like the shattering of icicles
In the wind.

## Dictionary

O sassafras, your portrait in a book
Has made the letter S a pitcher of dew,
Has made the years fall open at the blessings,
And cut time's alphabet in two.

And there are no more words words, only
A piece of woodland coined with sun-in-dapple
And near my foot the three-times trillium leaf
And under her parasol the pale May-apple.

And I am standing halved by past and present,
Confused in light that's double like a shell,
Recalling the hermit thrush, his fine soprano
And that no other bird could hide so well.

Recalling maiden-hair in frail triangles,
And a little snake who had a yellow chin,
And Judas-tree with green hearts hung, so choicely,
And next year's beads of flowers tight within.

O sassafras, your portrait in a book
Has left my mind half-slanted and awry,
Tilted to eastward in a western land
To see the wind-flower tremble and hear
                    the whip-poor-will cry.

# Driving Clock

(Below Mt. Wilson Observatory)

O lovely wheel that weds along the groove
And wedless parts the shimmer of your rim
To silver singly in the tempered air,
You, slow as God, have overtaken Him.

O pale perimeter of grace, anointed
For that hypnotic glide impinged on might,
Who forged you on the anvil of the stars
And set you turning to the laws of light?

How cryptic is the calm, the intricate
Unindolence of power that knows its place,
So gravely balanced between pole and pole,
So local in the mystery of space.

Time is a solid here, co-bound and wrought
With matter's destiny.   Tell, who can tell
How period is lapped in pause of steel,
How truth is made to fit itself so well?


# Noon on Alameda Street

Sun, when it shines on traffic, has a look
Of loaded radiance that might explode,
Yet keeps its kindle like a meaning known
Only to motors in the city road,

Only to fury lifted of all horns
Mourning to themselves a thing to come,
For we have heard delirium in a claxon,
Seen revelation lit on chromium.

On Alameda Street the earth is turning
Secret among old sluices and their kind:
The voice of men among machines at noon
Comes like a sigh from history to the mind,

For in this noon there is no light like light,
(Oh, tell us, dark on asphalt, of the sun)
But brightness spawning upon dirty glass,
But fever smoking at meridian,

But men and women riding in their graves
With hands upon a wheel they cannot keep
Clear in the rapt confusion of the crowd,
Crowd and the fate of motion and of sleep.

# Slow Boone

Call it our land, our valley, but not ours
Got by our fathers' guns and Paiutes slain,
Until a slower haste of continent
Wins twice to west across the brimming plain.

O quick compatriots, now is the need
To reap a secret in the acre sealed
Untouched by prairie rage or primitive.
Say truth is deeper than the battlefield.

Say all sure things that frenzy overtakes
Win to the greenest goal by their own powers.
Say patience like the burning of a rock
Turns passion, then will the land be ours.

Then will the native heart be cleared for use,
The horny miles run inward to the mind
And the blood's visionary length at last
Be in the poet's actual vein refined.

His then a continent to sensitize,
His the blue land not plowed by pioneers,
His the last newcoming the plains will know,
A slow Boone quietly fingering frontiers.

# Prayer for This Day

Here, west of winter, lies the ample flower
Along a bough not builded on by snow.
Now earth conceives the bridal and the bower.
Now what was rain is vistas in a row
Of spring, or miles of water knocking upon stone.
The random green heals over without flaw,
Hills heave a bright front to the midmost sun.
Oh, what are we to say that worlds are lost
Or what bears heaviest on the heart almost?

Still to a century superb for death
The emerald shrub again, the rose undwindled,
Still quail are whistling with a bubble's breath
And lean and tender lilies taper still,
Still satin moths at night with great eyes kindled
Throb into flame.  If there is time to will
Prayer from a heart too long by reason fondled,
Then here where flinty branches loosen into white,
Here at the balmy side of spring's re-birth
Kneel down.  We ask no vision, no heavenly light,
But simple faith, like faith of grass, in earth,
And seed's old dream against the night, the night.

# 12 O'Clock Freight

Away, four miles, I heard the Santa Fe
Go down the track, and I could see the sight,
A freighter pulling out with cryptic cars,
So sealed and sullen in the flowered night.

At home and in my mind I saw her draw
Her secrets where black fences line the rail,
And choking orange groves abandoned to
No rain and flaky pestilence of scale.

And then by palmy drives and boulevards
Where stucco gleams beside the carob-tree,

And Spanish patios in vain enclose
Lone hearts from Iowa and Kankakee.

And past Anita's wealthy meadows where
Her smouldering pea-cocks doze among her hounds
With sapphire laces folded in the dark
That daily trail and twitch about the grounds.

On by the oaks whose forest stoops upon
The listing hills where once the drift of deer
Drew down with winter's waters green,
A herd of dreams in glassy atmosphere.

Here comes, she comes, here comes the glooming train
Flying her bloody smoke.   People in bed
Rouse halfway, and made lonely at the sound
Touch hands and touch their hands to a dear head.

And tell me, night, the names of all the men
Who ride the freight train, stretched upon the cars,
Heavy and motherless and rockasleep,
Their hungry faces pointed at the stars.

What destiny, dark suburb, what asylum
Of rot will they slip off into at last,
When on the final freighter, oh caboose,
The ruby jerk and leer of light go past?

Into the valley, long San Gabriel,
The train crawls bleak and moaning down the track,
And from the rail the starlight spurts again
With sudden gush of brightness after black.

# Smith Brothers' Lumber Shed

Here in the shadow of the Smiths, my forest,
The flower of Oregon is straight and dead,
The pine that whistled and the cedar's harp,
A silent lumber counted in a shed.
So many miles, so many winds between
This corner south, your sable forest north,

*

Where loud you rolled your branches on the storm,
Slow begot new green, slow brought it forth.
O Mr. Smith, O Oregon, I saw
All that you both possess under one shed,
The earth profoundly holding up her trees,
And every man, a home upon his head.
And more, believe, I saw and counted most
The northern stars still trembling through the branch
And far below, the pale glass of a flower,
And I forebore to pick it up so blanche.
It is for Mr. Smith, he must be laid
Sometimes limpid among lengths of lumber,
Heaving his eye up to remembered shade,
Hearing the lovely voice of living timber,
And see—it's natural, not as a Smith possessed—
His fir-trees drinking at the snow's fine breast.

# Swift Love, Sweet Motor

And will they always be so tender, her
Face a kind of star to burn him up, she
Nearly there and wholly tremulous, his lap?
Where ecstacy lolls unabashed, his knee?

Will always run the road under the wheels,
The kiss of tire to boulevard complete,
The fuels of joy and speed flow brightly, make
Sunday combust in a miraculous heat?

Will ever just this perilous hot way
Survive to make them almost crash in bliss,
Just missing (where old panic licks his grin)
Black flowers and funerals of the abyss?

Question to question: and no answer mine.
Love rides locked to love whose motors pass
Leaving upon my traffic eye one token,
A gleam at fifty miles through shatterproof glass,

Her smile, a little honey-comb just broken.

# Gwendolen Haste

## *from Montana Wives*

# The Ranch in the Coulee

He built the ranch house down a little draw,
So that he should have wood and water near.
The bluffs rose all around.   She never saw
The arching sky, the mountains lifting clear;
But to the west the close hills fell away
And she could glimpse a few feet of the road.
The stage to Roundup went by every day,
Sometimes a rancher town-bound with his load,
An auto swirling dusty through the heat,
Or children trudging home on tired feet.

At first she watched it as she did her work,
A horseman pounding by gave her a thrill,
But then within her brain began to lurk
The fear that if she lingered from the sill
Someone might pass unseen.   So she began
To keep the highroad always within sight,
And when she found it empty long she ran
And beat upon the pane and cried with fright.
The winter was the worst.   When snow would fall
He found it hard to quiet her at all.

# Prairie Wolf

North of the house there was a graveled range of hills,
Stubborn and bare with clinging grey dry grass,
Where, resting sometimes through her vacant days, she watched
The far swift shadows of the coyotes pass.

She told herself her life was like those stony hills,
Unfertile, bitter in the blaze of noon,
Where fearful yellow shapes slipped by uncertainly
And wailed for sorrow underneath the moon.

# The Reason

She told them when they came and found him there
That he had tried to kill her with the knife—
Although she knew that he would never dare
To threaten her—much less to take her life.
So they who had seen his rages let her go.
But brooding on it in the later years
She felt she might have stood each curse and blow,
His shouting anger or his brutal jeers,
But on that day her heart was tired and sore
With God's austere and high indifference.
She saw the withered fields beyond the door,
The rotting barns, the filth, the broken fence,
And all her faded days, robbed of delight,
Where everything but weariness had fled,
So when he came in lowering that night
She took the rabbit gun and shot him dead.


# The Mocker

The cowboy comes to town
Scornful.
He wears his orange wool chaps,
And scarlet handkerchief,
And embroidered boots;
Under him is his beautiful silver-mounted
    saddle.
He meets his friends down by the tracks
In a huddle of old buildings
That were there before the railroad.
But sometimes he rides his pony out on Spencer
    Avenue.
He digs his spurs in the pony's side,
And the pony bucks,
And the cowboy whoops most insolent and con-
    temptuous
Outside the fine brick residence of the President

        *

of the First State Bank.
Almost the cowboy would urge his pony over the
     brick coping among the shrubbery and
     perennials
But that sacrilege is forbidden—
Even to cowboys.

# The Stoic

She guessed there wasn't any time for tears
Because her heart had held them all unshed
While one by one her little hopes had fled
Down through those racking, windy, drouth-filled years,
The frozen winter when the cattle died,
The year the hail bent flat the tender wheat,
The thirsty summers with their blazing heat—
She met them all with wordless, rigid pride.

But when, sometimes, the children in the spring
Searching through barren hill or ragged butte,
Would heap her lap with loco blooms, and bring
Clouds of blue larkspur and bright bitter-root,
Then would she run away to hide her pain
For memory of old gardens drenched with rain.

# Prayer of the Homesteader

Dear Lord, we are afraid.
We do not know this land.
These mountains are too cold and tall and bare.
Within their flanks the grey wolf has his lair.
Safety lay thick upon the fields
And friendly hilltops of our youth.
Lord, you will understand,
We are not cowards,
But we do not like this land.

We were taught simple things when we were young.
We know the path a plow makes in black loam,
The way of pleasant showers on April days,
The soft winds of our home.
We know the healing rains of summer nights,
And the gold plenty of the harvesting.
But this land fights.
Its hard brown sod protests against the plow,
Its stubborn grasses cling.
Our young crops are beat flat by roaring hail,
And when the rains should visit us in spring
There comes a hot strange gale,
Like desert wind blown over glittering sand
That dries the little wheat.
Lord, did you mean that men should farm this land?

Lord, this is not a land where men should live.
Our minds rake up a harvest of old tales
Whispered around old fires,
And butte and coulee ring with chattering wails.
Upon these iron benches Things have stalked.
When morning breaks we are afraid to look
For fear great feet have walked
And left crushed tracks upon the buffalo grass.
These creeping nights of ghosts were never made
For man and sleep.
Dear Lord, we are afraid.

Lord, can it be that this is not your land?
Your ways are peaceful ways through country lanes,
But you have never walked upon these plains,
We never see your face beneath these skies.
Come to us, Lord.
Man should not live alone within the world;
He is not strong nor wise.
Bless our thin crops.
Teach the small trees to grow.
Stretch us your kindly hand.
We must have comfort in this alien land.

# Dorchester Plate

Bound with blue where thirteen stars
space demurely, crowned by an eagle,
flecked with marionettes under stiff trees,
the past climbs to an easy hill.

When could years have shown thus—
glazed—circular?  Yet grandfathers of living
women darkened this grass with death,
sweated through that voiceless mill.

So soon does blood shrink to
the dimensions of a shelf.  The gaudy tones
of passion spill at last on
this cycle of pottery—this mirror of the unreal.

# Janet Lewis

## Country Burial

After the words of the magnificence and doom,
After the vision of the splendor and the fear,
They go out slowly into the flowery meadow,
Carrying the casket, and lay it on the earth
By the grave's edge.   The daisies bend and straighten
Under the trailing skirts, and serious faces
Look with faint relief, and briefly smile.
Into this earth the flesh and wood shall melt
And under these familiar common flowers
Flow through the earth they both have understood
By sight and touch and daily sustenance.
And this is comforting;
For heaven is a blinding radiance where
Leaves are no longer green, nor water wet,
Milk white, soot black, nor winter weather cold,
And the eyeless vision of the Almighty Face
Brings numbness to the untranslatable heart.

## Girl Help

Mild and slow and young,
She moves about the room,
And stirs the summer dust
With her wide broom.

In the warm, lofted air,
Soft lips together pressed,
Soft wispy hair,
She stops to rest,

And stops to breathe,
Amid the summer hum,
The great white lilac bloom
Scented with days to come.

# Winter Garden

Child, dream of a pomegranate tree
Weighted with ruby, showered with gold,
Dream of a fig tree under the cold
And cloudy sky
Lifting its curved and silver boughs
Like a roofless house
For birds that be
Tardily in November here;
Dream of a spare
And twisted vine—
The grape—and ivy for the hair,
And honeysuckle, stubborn twine;
And of the firm and hidden shape
Of the green orange deep in the tree;
And dreaming, in my garden be.
      I have bestowed calendulas
That brighten beside reddening haws,
And rooted out the hoarhound grey,
And pulled the nettle from our way,
And torn my hand on bramble berry.
Then, if a drop, red as a cherry,
Of blood upon my finger show,
It is a seal set to a vow
To ward and to cherish even as now,
Now that you sleep your joy to replenish,
Each branch, each varied lifting bough,
That not a leaf in your garden perish.


# Lines with a Gift of Herbs

The summer's residue
In aromatic leaf,
Shrunken and dry, yet true
In fragrance, their belief,

These from the hard earth drew
Essence of rosemary,
Lavender, faintly blue,
While unconfused nearby

From the same earth distilled
Grey sage and savory,
Each one distinctly willed—
Stoic morality.

The Emperor said, "Though all
Conspire to break thy will,
Clear stone, thou emerald, shall
Be ever emerald still."

And these, small, unobserved,
Through summer chemistry,
Have all their might conserved
In treasure, finally.

# The Hangar at Sunnyvale: 1937

Above the marsh, a hollow monument,
Ribbed with aluminum, enormous tent
Sheeted with silver, set to face the gale
Of the steady wind that filled the clipper sail,
The hangar stands.   With doors now buckled close
Against the summer wind, the empty house
Reserves a space shaped to the foundered dream.
The Macon, lost, moves with the ocean stream.

Level the marshes, far and low the hills.
The useless structure, firm on the ample sills,
Rises incredible to state again:
Thus massive was the vessel, built in vain.
For this one purpose the long sides were planned
To lines like those of downward pouring sand,
Time-sifting sand; but Time immobile, stayed,
In substance bound, in these bright walls delayed.

This housed the shape that plunged through stormy air.
Empty cocoon!   Yet was the vision fair
That like a firm bright cloud moved from the arch,
Leaving this roof to try a heavenly march;
Impermanent, impractical, designed
To frame a paradox and strongly bind
The weight, the weightless in a living shape
To cruise the sky and round the cloudy Cape.

Less substance than a mathematic dream
Locked in the hollow keel and webbèd beam!
Of the ingenious mind the expensive pride,
The highest hope, the last invention tried!
And now the silver tent alone remains.
Slowly the memory of disaster wanes.
Still in the summer sun the bastions burn
Until the inordinate dream again return.

# Peggy Pond Church

## Sheep Country

In spring the sheep are driven over the mountain
While there is still snow knee-deep in every shadow
And the wind's edge is sharp in the Valle country.
The sheep come up from the canyons
Like a grey cloud.  They move slowly.  They leave unnibbled
Not a low-growing leaf, not a sliver of grass,
Not a flower.

In Capulin canyon the river crossings are muddied
Before the wild choke cherries are in flower;
There are a hundred twisted trails on Rabbit mountain
Made by the sheep that come up from Peña Blanca,
From Cienega and Cochiti, from Santo Domingo,
From the dirty corrals, from the flat, dusty mesas
Where they have fed all winter.

I have seen them going up Santa Clara canyon in April
When Tsacoma mountain is still a white cloud of brightness
Lifted against the sky; when the wind is bitter
And there is only a haze of green around the aspens
You can see by looking slantwise, never directly,
Never in a second glance, never by coming closer.

I have seen the sheep move up Santa Clara canyon
And over the ridge
And down the Rito de los Indios and onward into
The long, curved Valle San Antonio.

And I have seen the names of the sheepherders written
On the aspen trees halfway up Tsacoma
And on Redondo mountain where the aspens fight for their rootholds
In the black rocks, in the frozen lava.
Casimiro Chaves, I have seen written; Juan Pino; Reyes Contreras;
From Chamita and Abiquiu and Española,
Nambé and Pojuaque.

These are the names of boys, carved here and written,
Whose wits, they say, aren't fit for any other work,
Or men whose minds are still the minds of children;
Who do not desire anything more of living
Than to lie in the glittering shadow of an aspen
On the rim of the Valles where the sheep feed
And move downward slowly.

There are men who desire much more and find much less.
Must we all be madmen, I wonder, or innocents,
To follow the sheep along the ridge of the Valles,
Looking down, west, to the sea of grasses,
    The far-off, tangled, grass-hidden threads of water,
And the nets of rain through which the farther mountains
Shine like a shadow?

# Abiquiu—Thursday in Holy Week

Is there any way I can be sure to remember
Abiquiu?
How the sun went down suddenly
Behind the hills, and the river darkened.    Everything
Became sound only laid upon silence
        where had been lately
Bright houses and people moving past them,
        and dogs and children.

The moon was a long time coming up.
It came up slowly.
The hills grew tall and terrible before it.    The long mesa
Behind Abiquiu was a huge blackness, growing blacker
On the slow silver sky.
The fields had been ploughed a little and we stumbled
        through them
Guiding our steps by grasping the budding willows
Beside the acequia.    We didn't belong here.
This wasn't our world.    We should never have come
        here at all.
We shivered and laid our lengths along the border

•

70

Of the field, a wall of low stone.  The trail from
         the morada
Went past that wall.  We heard something wailing
High in the hills.  We waited.

A little beyond midnight they came out of the morada
And went past the wall, three of them, one singing;
One with the pito, the Penitente flute that is
         more sorrowful
Than any sorrowful sound that was ever uttered
In music.  The third man marched
With body bent a little forward.  At the end
         of each line of singing
He brought the woven whip across his shoulders
With a lashing sound, rhythmical, like an accent;
A sound that was dull and harsh, as though already
Blood softened the lean back.  A lantern flickered
In the hand of the singer.  Its swinging shadow
Was swallowed soon in darkness.

I, under the cold stars, there in the cold night, watching
This greatest of remembered tragedies enacted
By men who as soon as Easter was over
Would go back to their ordinary way of living—
To the fields they must finish plowing and sowing;
To the sheep that would be lambing soon in the canyons;
To the ditches that must be cleared to flood
         the orchards,
Each man when his turn came, from the mother
         acequia—
Men whose brown, wind-lined faces I had often
         seen passing
In wagons loaded with wood brought down
         from the mesas

Behind Abiquiu, or driving burros
Slowly, as if in some other country, along the highway.
I, crouched there against the cold stone, prone
         on the cold earth, listening,
Thought:  There is something they know, these men,
         that we have forgotten;

                    *

They remember, here in these mountains, here
    at Abiquiu on this spring night,
On this unforgettable Thursday before Easter,
That to imitate simply, unaware even of any
    special meaning
A great and tragic action, is to be lifted by it
For a moment out of commonplace living
    toward greatness.

# After Looking into a Genealogy

Time is not, when I remember you, my grandmothers.
Your bones, your flesh have gone into the dust;
From granite stones the wind has wiped your names.
The years have trod your graves flat with the earth,
You who were beautiful, you who died still young
In childbirth, you who saw
Ninety and more full years before you passed,
Whose husbands died at sea, whose husbands died
In the stern winters of a wilderness.

Time is not, when I remember you, my grandmothers.
Mercy and Lydia and Abigail,
Ruth and Mehitable; sea-captains' wives,
Daughters of soldiers, mothers of men of God;
Statira, Betsey, Patience, Margery,
Remember, whose other name the gravestones have forgotten.

Out of old books these names, from moldering stones,
All that is left of you, my grandmothers!
    All but the blood
That makes me one with you.   The blood that cried
Like a wanderer returned when I first saw—
I, the desert-born, this offspring
    of New England growing
Among New Mexico mountains—when I first saw
The dogwood blossoming in Connecticut woods,
The meadows sprinkled with a rain of daisies,
The apple-orchard set in low, green hills.

I know now why in my dreams I had seen those hills
        and had remembered
The covered bridges over Vermont rivers,
And why, whenever I came upon a clearing
        in mountain country
I thought:   One could build a house here.
That slope would make a pasture.   An orchard
        would be fruitful
In a few years, and the apples fragrant.
The butter I'd churn would be cool and sweetened
In a stone house over this mountain-spewed
        thread of water.

When I was a little girl
My mother kept the milk in a house
        built half underground
With shelves around the walls.   There the warm milk
        yellowed
With heavy cream in rows of shallow pans.   Something
        familiar,
Something not remembered first stirred in me
When I crept down to watch her.

But most of all, my grandmothers, your blood leaps
        in me
(Obliterating time, making of me one person with my
        forebears,
One person who has lived since life crawled up
        from the waters
And became man, who will not die
Till the last woman of this race is barren);
Most of all, my blood stirs with your voices
When the winds of winter thunder like ocean water
And the white snow whirls down in utter darkness.

Then I remember, or it seems as if I remembered,
The earliest winter, and the fierce grey water
Heaped between us and England (the grey water
Cradling more than one of my grandfathers),
The desperate stand we made against that winter,
The bitter battle.

We were sturdy-limbed, the daughers of that winter.
We had inherited strength that must be tried.
    We could not
Live and grow old, unrestless, in security,
And so we went off, should to shoulder with our men,
    and singing,
Into the farther wilderness.

In these days, my grandmothers, the weak live easily.
The weak crowd out the strong like weeds
    in an untilled garden.
Where can we go, we in whom your blood sings?—
The eager blood of our forefathers, of our foremothers,
    who marched chin forward
And always toward the horizon?

# The Nuclear Physicists

These are the men who
working secretly at night and against great odds
and in what peril they knew not of their own souls
invoked for man's sake the most ancient archetype of evil
and bade this go forth and save us at Hiroshima
and again at Nagasaki.

We had thought the magicians were all dead, but this was the
    blackest of magic.
There was even the accompaniment of fire and brimstone,
the shape of evil, towering leagues high into heaven
in terrible, malevolent beauty, and, beneath, the bare trees
made utterly leafless in one instant, and the streets where no
    one
moved, and some walls still standing
eyeless, and as silent as before Time.

These are the men who
now with aching voices
and with eyes that have seen too far into the world's fate,
tell us what they have done and what we must do.
                        •

In words that conceal apocalypse they warn us
what compact with evil was signed in the name of all the
    living,
and how, if we demand that Evil keep his bargain,
we must keep ours, and yield our living spirits
into the irrevocable service of destruction.

Now we, in our wilderness, must reject the last temptation:
the kingdoms of earth and all the power and the glory,
and bow before the Lord our God, and serve Him
whose still small voice, after the wind, the earthquake,
the vision of fire, still speaks to those who listen
and will the world's good.

# For the Hippolytus of Euripides

Like a gaunt pillar wreathed in weeping flowers
so stands in memory the afternoon
I first saw played the Greek Hippolytus.
Euripides, your ageless spirit stood
motionless at my side, and through your eyes
I saw the dreadful beauty of that doom
rise like a wave from the unfathomed sea
in which all passion sleeps.  I saw it move
with gathering weight of agony and tears
upon that king and on that ravaged queen,
and on that lovely and ill-cherished youth
flung harsh on death.  I heard the dark wave moan
and saw the delicate maidens lean like flowers
against the cold, the imperturbable stone.
Euripides, you knew what we must know
and what we dare not know:  that life is stern
beyond our power to make it what we will,
and that the gods use men for their own ends,
and that the other face of love is hate.
That we can do so is what makes us men
and more than innocent flowers or mindless birds
that bloom or fly and perish without heed.
This is man's greatness, to behold his fate

unswerving as a wave, strong as the sea,
nor yet to stand aside, nor shield his eyes
but with his whole heart and with all his mind
to praise this beauty even though he dies.

# Elegy for Another Day

Walking at evening along the edge of the loma
at the hour of daylight ebbing, the lamps being lighted,
I came past corrals where the tame beasts had been bedded,
stirring like children not yet asleep, left lonely.

The domestic fires of day dreamed down into soft ash;
only earth's west rim still glowed like an ember.
The twilight arch curved upward on the eastern
sky like the shadow of receding daylight.

Humans, companioned with one another in warm houses,
like bees hived in winter, had left the earth to silence,
as though sleep should heal the memory of violence,
as though maternal night made all things brothers,

as though earth had not received the blood of Abel,
as though men shared the breast of their one mother,
nor dreamed one might be loved above another,
nor fallen to quarreling yet who should be greatest.

A woman was standing, quiet, by the gate of the sheep pen
blessing with a last look the creatures she had tended,
alone and with peace in her eyes, the long day ended,
untired and strong like an eternal being

who knows her children will come home at evening
weary of warfare, all their weapons broken,
to sleep, to dream the word that must be spoken,
and wake perhaps embraced as still in dreaming.

# Nellie Burget Miller

## The Woman in the Field

With gnarled hands folded on her idle hoe
She stands and stares until the train has slipped
Over the grade and out of sight.   What dreams
Of sudden flight does it arouse?   What hope
Is left her of escape?   One with the soil
She seems, her shapeless garments' faded brown
Serves for protective coloring, and Life
Has broken her to satisfy some urge
As she in turn breaks up the patient clod.

She does not speak, for dumbness long ago
Closed those thin lips to all but daily need;
Hard words she has for grim necessity,
But none to spare for beauty; her days still hold
Two things of interest—the train—and sleep.

That passive scarecrow in her rust-stained field
Set deep, stiff arms akimbo, motionless—
Had dreams and visions once before Fate set
This seal upon her uncomplaining lips;
Dumbly she stirs her ashen altar fire,
*Her tragedy lies not in things she missed*
*But that she lost desire.*

## The Sun Drops Red

The sun drops red through a curtain of dust,
White scars seam the alkali plain,
No sound or motion—save over there
A tumbleweed starts on its endless quest
For God knows what—or where.
The brown grass clings to the fields like rust,
But deep in my heart is the sound of rain—
The stealthy moccasined feet of the rain,

•

Pat, pat, on the sun-baked crust;
Like dear remembered dreams of love
In sleepless nights of pain.
The sun drops red through a curtain of dust.

# The Ploughman

His father taught him how to hold the plough
And turn black furrows straight, with eye
Unswerving, to the forty's edge; but now
He ploughs a curving edge; when winds are high
His topsoil holds.   And now he leaves a strip
Between the beans and winter wheat—fallow
For next year's seeding.   The fecund earth must skip
A year to build her strength, lest soil go shallow.

He ploughs a curving line because he knows
This sandy soil is not his father's loam;
And men have learned new ways—but when he goes
At sunset down the rutted track toward home
He thinks old thoughts—his father now long dead
Once thought—of woman, waiting food, and bed.

# Moon of the Springing Grass

There is a little hollow
between the river and the hill,
set thick with violets
in the moon of springing grass,
where strolling lovers sometimes come
to sit awhile and watch the robins foraging.

The place is silent and remote
as some lost Eden,
only the lovelorn note
of a hoot owl from the distant wood
or the swishing sound
of cattle, kneedeep in the gap,
accents the solitude.

A fisherman upon the farther bank
beneath the willows
where the black bass sleep,
draws up his line with quick resounding slap
and slowly makes for home.
The scent of burning leaves is on the air
and everywhere is the hum of bees—
The moon of springing grass has come.

# Italian Spring, 1945

O God of global battle-lines
Hold back the latent spring until
His tortured feet at last shall stand
Secure upon some sunlit plain,
Lest our hearts break at scent of plum
   Or lilacs shimmering after rain.

Spring has no meaning now and time
Is but a flux of agonies
As he plods on—step after step—
   Sunk deep in reddened snow and slime.

O grant this year brief armistice
From crocus carnivals and flocks
Of painted tulips in the park—
Lest our hearts break, remembering
   How he crawls upward in the dark.

# Peggy Simson Curry

## Ridge in Wind

A ridge in wind is clean,
As though the grass were brush-stroked white
Instead of custom green.
Even the sage is tinged with light
Where leaves were shuffled inside out
And dripped their color like a water spout.

A ridge in wind is strong,
Showing the bones of rimrock thrust
Skyward and sharp and long,
Wearing like armor all the rust
Of centuries and all the song—
As though the wind had taken time
To shape the high, clean land in rhyme.

## Driving Down from the Big Horns

I would like to keep this always:
Driving down from the Big Horn Mountains,
Down from the wind-cooled summer range—
Down to hills to lesser hills to plains—
Drifting into evening, humid and gold and strange,
Drawing the mountains down and drawing
Down the sky, wake-like and water-green,
Tilting the mountains over, tilting the sky
In long slow-curving like a river wheel
Feeble with time that lifts a river, lifts it up
And turns and turns it down—even as the heart
Now turns the mountains, sky and sun in flight
To one vast arc of flowing earth and light.

But motion carries me beyond the dream
Conceived in moving and I feel
The mountains heavy—straining back.
Where should I have stopped and stood
Surrendered to that perfect arc—
When did my mind betray me over
To the flat earth and the dark?

# Fishing at Sunrise

I stand where water sweeps between my knees.
Morning moves west across the fading sky
And Venus dims her pale, green lamp;
But here the Platte runs east with light,
Plunging toward canyons deep with night.

Wary of sun the shabby hills shrink back,
And where fast water breaks to quiet pools
I toss the bright fly out to drift the wind.
Over the rocks ripples spill liquid gold;
I wade hip-deep in gilded waves of cold.

Comes now the rush of shadow-shape, the leap
From green-white foam.   The frail rod bends
To frantic shaking of the line and hook
Till long and beautiful the great trout lies
And sun-up lays red beads upon his eyes.

# Lupine Ridge

Long after we are gone,
Summer will stroke this ridge in blue;
The hawk still flies above the flowers,
Thinking, perhaps, the sky has fallen
And back and forth forever he may trace
His shadow on its azure face.

Long after we are gone,
Evening wind will languish here
Between the lupine and the sage
To die a little death upon the earth,
As though over the sundown prairies fell
A requiem from a bronze-tongued bell.

Long after we are gone,
This ridge will shape the night,
Lifting the wine-streaked west,
Shouldering the stars.   And always here
Lovers will walk under the summer skies
Through flowers the color of your eyes.

# Red Butte in Autumn

Wind, wind I hear you walking by, I hear
The grass trail thin brown beads
Across the troubled earth.
I see the red butte rise like an old buffalo
Enraged by arrow wounds and charge
The sagging sky and throw
The crouched horizon back until a crack of blue
Breaks open—and the birds go through.

# Biobibliographies

Bibliographies may consist of two sections: the author's poetical works are included in Part I; if there are notable critical writings about the author's poetry, they will be listed in Part II.

## Eliza R. Snow (b. 1804-d. 1887)

Eliza Snow, born in Massachusetts, was at the age of two part of a pioneering move to Portage County, Ohio, a move which prefigured the migrations of the rest of her life. Precocious in school—she presented to her perplexed instructors homework assignments in verse—she did not submit her first poem for publication until she was twenty-two, and then under a pseudonym. The arrival of Joseph Smith (whom she later married) and Mormonism in her area turned Eliza's life's direction without markedly altering her character. Her poetry became celebration of the Mormon restoration and apologetics of their doctrine. "Though deep'ning trials throng your way,/ Press on, press on, ye saints of God," she wrote as she journeyed with the Latter-day Saints through their forced migrations from Ohio to Missouri, from Missouri to Illinois (where Smith was murdered), from Illinois to Utah. At each period of the hegira, Eliza, "Zion's Poetess," as the Mormons had titled her, celebrated her new-found faith in hymnlike verses, many of which are still sung in congregations of the Latter-day Saints. The most famous of these is "O My Father," included here under its original title "Invocation, or the Eternal Father and Mother." In Utah, Eliza, then wife in plural marriage to Brigham Young, rose to prominence as undisputed leader of Mormon women, heading three organizations of women and taking a leading role in business, charitable, and political enterprises. She published in all nine volumes, two of poetry, one biography, and several instructional books, as well as almost monthly speeches and occasional poems in newspapers.

I.  ***Eliza R. Snow An Immortal: Selected Writings of Eliza R. Snow.*** Salt Lake City: Nicholas G. Morgan, Sr., Foundation, 1957. (Contains an altered version of "Acrostic for Anna Geen." The version of the poem printed in this anthology is taken from the holograph copy of the poem found in Snow's *Diaries* in the Henry E. Huntington Library, San Marino, California. Copy courtesy of Maureen Ursenbach Beecher.)
***Poems: Religious, Historical and Political***, I. Liverpool, England: F. D. Richards, 1856.
***Poems: Religious, Historical and Political***, II. Salt Lake City: L.D.S. Printing and Publishing Establishment, 1877.

II. Beecher, Maureen Ursenbach. "The Eliza Enigma: The Life and Legend of Eliza R. Snow." In *Charles Redd Monographs in Western History, No. 6, Essays on the American West, 1974-1975*. Provo, Utah: Brigham Young University Press, 1976. Reprinted in *Dialogue: A Journal of Mormon Thought*, 11, No. 1 (Spring 1978).

-----. "Eliza R. Snow," In *Mormon Sisters: Women in Early Utah*. Cambridge, Massachusetts: Emmeline Press, 1976.

Larsen, Cindy Lesser. "Whoever Heard of a Utah Poet? An Overview Of Poetry in the Early Church." *Century 2* (Fall 1979), pp. 32-61.

### Ina Coolbrith (b. 1841-d. 1928)

Eliza R. Snow's niece, Josephine Donna Smith, was born in Illinois and came west by wagon at 10, a member of the first party through Beckwourth Pass into California. In the little town of Los Angeles, where her family settled, her first poems were published. Here, at 17, she married Robert Carsley and, at 21, after a tumultuous relationship, divorced him. After her divorce, she moved north to San Francisco and changed her name to Ina Coolbrith. In the Bay area, Coolbrith's literary reputation was established. She came to associate with the leading literary luminaries of the day: Mark Twain, Ambrose Bierce, John Muir, Bret Harte and others. Her elegy for Byron, "With a Wreath of Laurel," hand-carried by the flamboyant Joaquin Miller to the grave of the English poet, caused an international sensation—and brought about a critical reappraisal of Byron. She was a regular contributor to the West's foremost periodicals, was selected Oakland's first librarian, and published three volumes of verse. Surviving San Francisco's disastrous earthquake and fire of 1906, Coolbrith was appointed California's poet laureate in 1915, the first female laureate in America.

I. *A Perfect Day*. San Francisco: [John H. Carmany,] 1881.
*Songs from the Golden Gate*. Boston and New York: Houghton, Mifflin, 1895.
*Wings of Sunset*. Boston and New York: Houghton Mifflin, 1929.

II Rhodehamel, Josephine and Raymond Wood. *Ina Coolbrith*. Provo, Utah: Brigham Young University Press, 1973.

### Ella Higginson (b. circa 1860-d. 1941)

Born in Kansas and raised in La Grande in eastern Oregon, Ella Mae Rhoads married a pharmacist and spent most of the rest of her life in Bellingham, Washington, where she wrote one novel (*Mariella, of Out-West*), numerous award-winning short stories, and six collections of verse. Higginson was an inveterate club woman, and selections of her published and unpublished poems were collected in a posthumous edition by the Washington State Federation of Women's Clubs in 1941. Included in their anthology is "Four-Leaf Clover," the poem still taught to young people involved in 4-H. Higginson's lyrics were admired by her contemporaries: over fifty composers set her words to music; her songs were sung by the early 20th century's greatest singers, Calvé, Caruso, and McCormack.

I.   *A Bunch of Western Clover*. New Whatcom, Washington: Edson and Irish Printers, 1894.
*Four-Leaf Clover*. Bellingham, Washington: Edson and Irish, 1894.
*From the Land of the Snow Pearls*. New York: Macmillan, 1897.
*The Vanishing Race and Other Poems*. Bellingham, Washington: Sherman, 1911.
*The Voice of April Land*. New York: Macmillan, 1903.
*When the Birds Go North Again*. New York: Macmillan, 1898.

II.   Reynolds, Helen Louise. "Ella Higginson, Northwest Author." Unpublished Master's thesis, University of Washington, 1941.
Washington State Federation of Women's Clubs, ed. *Ella Higginson ...A Tribute*. Bellingham, Washington: Union Printing Co., 1941.

**Sharlot Mabridth Hall** (b. 1870-d. 1943)

Westering with her family to Arizona from Kansas in the early 1880's, Sharlot Hall was thrown from her horse and suffered a serious, lingering spine injury which, in the '90's, confined her to bed. During this period she began writing. Throughout the next twenty years, at the urging and with the advice of her mother, Hall wrote her best poems. In addition, she managed two ranches (hers and her parents') wrote for and edited Charles F. Lummis' magazine *Land of Sunshine* (later retitled *Out West*), served as Arizona's Territorial Historian (the first woman in the state to hold public office), and undertook various historical projects and expeditions (see her recently published diary, *Sharlot Hall on the Arizona Strip*). Later, she would found what is now the Sharlot Hall Historical Society and Museum in Prescott, Arizona. In 1910, in Boston, her first volume of poems, *Cactus and Pine*, was published. It received enthusiastic reviews and sold out. In her valuable "Preface" to the second edition of this volume (Phoenix, 1924), Hall expresses her Western loyalties and also relates how this edition came to be. Noting that the plates of the Boston edition had been melted down in a WWI munitions factory and were "shot at the Hun," Hall wryly proposes that her poems have "done their part in winning the war in a decidedly original way for poetry."

I.   *Cactus and Pine*. Boston: Sherman, French & Co., 1911.
     *Cactus and Pine*. 2nd, rev. ed. Phoenix, Arizona Republican Print
     Shop, 1924.
     *Poems of a Ranch Woman*. [Josephine MacKenzie, comp. Sharlot
     Hall Historical Society,] 1953.
II.  Weston, James J. "Sharlot Hall: Arizona's Pioneer Lady of Litera-
     ture," *Journal of the West*, IV, 4 (October 1965), 539-552.


**Alice Corbin** (b. 1881-d. 1949)

Missouri-born Alice Corbin saw her first book of poems published while she
attended high school in Chicago in 1898. By 1912, after having married
William P. Henderson, a Boston art instructor, in 1905, and having given
birth to Alice Olive, their one child, in 1907, Corbin was chosen by Harriet
Monroe to be Assistant Editor for *Poetry: A Magazine of Verse*. In this
position she is usually credited with having "discovered" Edgar Lee
Masters and Carl Sandburg. However, because her health was failing (she
suffered from tuberculosis), the Hendersons moved to Santa Fe in 1916
and Corbin's contributions to *Poetry* waned, although she and Monroe
co-edited the influential anthology, *The New Poetry*, in 1917 and Corbin's
name appeared on the masthead of *Poetry* until 1923. Corbin's first book
of Western poetry appeared in 1920. She edited one of the finest regional
collections, *The Turquoise Trail, An Anthology of New Mexico Poetry*,
in 1928. Five years later, her second volume of Western poetry appeared.
Thereafter, despite her fragile health, Corbin wrote a classic study of the
Southwestern religious cult, the Penitentes, served as editor-in-chief of the
New Mexico project of the American Guide series, was named librarian
and curator of the Museum of Navaho Ceremonial Art in Santa Fe, and
also lectured and advised young writers until her death in 1949.

I.   *Linnet Songs*. Chicago: Wind-Tryst Press, 1898.
     *Red Earth: Poems of New Mexico*. Chicago: Ralph Fletcher Sey-
     mour, 1920.
     *The Spinning Woman of the Sky*. Chicago: R. F. Seymour Co.,
     1912.
     *The Sun Turns West*. Santa Fe: Writers' Editions, 1933.
II.  Pearce, T. M. *Alice Corbin Henderson*. Southwest Writers Series,
     No. 21. Austin, Texas: Steck-Vaughn, 1969.


**Hazel Hall** (b. 1886-d. 1924)

Ben Hur Lampman notes in her obituary (*The Portland Oregonian*, 12

May 1924) that Hazel Hall was an invalid most of her life and that "to the hour of her last illness Miss Hall worked daily on poems that were to appear in her third volume.... Perhaps," he comments, "she was given some intuitive glimpse of the short span that remained in which to write, for it is singularly coincidental that at least two of these poems found their theme in death. One was called 'Riddle' and the last of all was named 'Slow Death'." Lampman goes on to quote these lines from Hall's last poem:

> You need no other death than this
> Slow death that wears your heart away;
> It is enough, the death that is
> Your every night, your every day.

Hall was born in St. Paul, Minnesota, and came as a child with her family to Portland, Oregon, where she lived out her life. Because of a fall or an attack of scarlet fever, she was unable to walk after the age of 12. Like the frequently invalided Sharlot Hall (no relation), Hazel Hall turned to writing when physically disabled. She saw her first poem published when she was 30, only to die eight years later.

I.  *Cry of Time*. New York: E. P. Dutton, 1928.
    *Curtains*. New York: John Lane, 1921.
    *Selected Poems*. Boise: Ahsahta Press, 1980.
    *Walkers*. New York: Dodd, Mead & Co., 1923.
II. Bentley, Beth. "Mirror in the Shadows: Hazel Hall, 1886-1924." *Concerning Poetry*, 13, No. 2 (Fall 1980), 7-12.
    Matthews, Eleanor H. "Hazel Hall." *Northwest Review*, XVII, Nos. 2-3 (1979), 98-103.
    Franklin, Viola Price. *A Tribute to Hazel Hall*. Caldwell, Idaho: Caxton, 1939.
    Saul, George Branson. *Quintet: Essays on Five American Women Poets*. The Hague: Mouton & Co., 1967.

**Mary Austin** (b. 1868-d. 1934)

Mary Hunter was born in Carlinville, Illinois, where she had a mystical experience at the age of 5, the first of many in a remarkable, colorful, dedicated life. Educated at Blackburn College in Illinois, she moved in 1888 to California, where she taught public school and married Stafford Austin in 1891. Two years later, their daughter, Ruth, was born brain-damaged; the same year, Mary's first story was accepted for publication. As her marriage dissolved over the next twenty years, Mary Austin found other pursuits:

she was associated with Jack London, George Sterling, and others in founding the literary colony at Carmel, California; her best prose works, *The Land of Little Rain* and *The Flock*, were published; she travelled to Rome, London, and New York, writing about and lecturing on feminism, mysticism, regionalism, politics, ethnic studies, etc. In 1914 she was reluctantly divorced by Stafford. Ruth died in the flu epidemic of 1918, and Mary immediately relocated in Santa Fe, although she spent much of her time in New York until 1924 when she made the southwest town her permanent residence. There she pursued her interests in Spanish-American culture, writing, and Native American poetics, making a singular contribution to the study of American poetics with the publication of *The American Rhythm*. Three years after her death, her ashes were buried on Mt. Picacho, east of Santa Fe.

I.   *The American Rhythm. Studies and Re-expressions of American Songs*. 1923, 1930; rpt. New York: Cooper Square Publishers, 1970.

     *Children Sing in the Far West*. Boston and New York: Houghton Mifflin, 1928.

II.  Lyday, Jo. W. *Mary Austin: The Southwest Works*. Southwestern Writers Series, No. 16. Austin, Texas: Steck-Vaughn, 1968.

     Pearce, T. M. *Mary Hunter Austin*. New York: Twayne Publishers, 1965.


**Genevieve Taggard** (b. 1894-d. 1948)

In the preface to her sixth book of poems, Genevieve Taggard writes bitterly about her birth and youth in Waitsburg, Washington, and glowingly of her early years spent near Honolulu, where her parents were public school teachers and missionaries for the Christian Church. It was on the Islands she began to write. In 1914 she entered the University of California at Berkeley and there, possibly because of her family's poverty and possibly because of the *Main Street*-mindedness of Waitsburg, she became involved with politics she has described as vaguely Socialistic and left-of-center. After graduation in 1919, she worked in a New York City publishing house, married Robert Wolf in 1921, and gave birth to a daughter. Taggard, a prolific writer of poetry and prose, had her first volume of verse published in 1922. She taught at various Eastern schools (Mt. Holyoke, Bennington, and Sarah Lawrence), won a Guggenheim Fellowship (1931), and was divorced from Wolf and married Kenneth Durant (1934 and 1935, respectively). Her later poetry is characterized by political overtones, but Taggard was consistently concerned with music and poetry of place. Like Ella Higginson's, many of Taggard's poems were set to music. And in her last volume of verse she lamented the lack of Hawaiian poetry, asserting, "A place that has not been truly felt and communicated does not, in a certain sense, exist."

I.  *Calling Western Union*. New York: Harper & Brothers, 1936.
    *Collected Poems 1918-1938*. New York: Harper & Brothers, 1938.
    *For Eager Lovers*. New York: Boni, 1922.
    *Hawaiian Hilltop*. San Francisco: Wycoff & Gelber, Lantern Press, 1923.
    *Long View*. New York: Harper & Brothers, 1942.
    *Not Mine To Finish: Poems 1928-1934*. New York: Harper & Brothers, 1934.
    *Origin: Hawaii; Poems*. Honolulu: Donald Angus, 1947.
    *A Part of Vermont*. East Jamaica, Vermont: The River Press, 1945.
    *Slow Music*. New York: Harper & Brothers, 1946.
    *To the Natural World*. Boise: Ahsahta Press, 1980.
    *Travelling Standing Still: Poems 1918-1928*. New York: Alfred A. Knopf, 1928.
    *Words for the Chisel*. New York: Alfred A. Knopf, 1926.

## Hildegarde Flanner (b. 1899-)

Hildegarde Flanner was born near Indianapolis, Indiana. She was educated at Sweet Briar College in Virginia and, like Genevieve Taggard, at the University of California at Berkeley. In 1926 she married the artist and architect Frederick Monhoff, who created illustrations for many of her books; other beautiful volumes by her were produced under the direction of Porter Garnett, one of America's most important typographic designers and printers: hers are among the loveliest of publications by a Western poet. Besides poetry, Flanner has written primarily essays, but she is also known for her articles and book reviews, as well as her one-act plays. Currently, the younger sister to Janet Flanner (of the **New Yorker**), lives in Calistoga, California, 75 miles north of San Francisco in vineyard country. Miss Flanner, an ardent conservationist and dedicated regionalist, will have a collection of old and new Western poems published by Ahsahta Press in 1979.

I.  *The Hearkening Eye*. Boise: Ahsahta Press, 1979.
    *If There Is Time*. Norfolk, Connecticut: New Directions, 1942.
    *In Native Light*. Calistoga, California: James E. Beard, 1970.
    *This Morning*. New York: F. Shay, 1921.
    *Time's Profile*. New York: Macmillan, 1929.

*A Tree in Bloom*. San Francisco: Lantern Press, 1924.
*Young Girl*. San Francisco: H. S. Crocker, 1920.

### Gwendolen Haste (b. 1889-d. 1979)

Even though she spent only ten or twelve years of her life in the West, Gwendolen Haste was a Western poet. Born in Illinois, she grew up in Wisconsin, graduated from the University of Chicago in 1912, and then helped her father edit *The Scientific Farmer*, first in Lincoln, Nebraska, and later in Billings, Montana. Most of her poems spring from her years in Montana. In the mid-1920's, Haste moved East permanently, first to join the editorial staff of *Survey* magazine and later to work with the Consumer Service Department of General Foods Corporation. She was the Secretary of the Poetry Society of America during 1928-1929 and remained on its board of directors until 1935. In 1936 she married Marlin Douglass Hennesey of Hillsboro, New Hampshire. Haste's poems have been published in numerous national magazines; one titled "The Ranch in the Coulee" won *The Nation* poetry prize in 1922. In 1930 her volume *Young Land* was published, and in 1976 Ahsahta Press issued her *Selected Poems*.

I.  *Selected Poems*. Boise: Ahsahta Press, 1976.
    *The Young Land*. New York: Coward-McCann, 1930.
II. Bangs, Carol Jane. "Women Poets and the 'Northwest School,'" in *Women, Women Writers, and the West* by L. L. Lee and Merrill Lewis. Troy, New York: Whitston, 1979. [Miss Haste's name is misspelled in this essay.]

### Janet Lewis (b. 1899-)

In 1923, for reasons of health, Janet Lewis left Chicago to move to Santa Fe, as Alice Corbin had done seven years earlier. There Lewis met the poet, professor, and critic Yvor Winters, who was recovering from tuberculosis, and married him in 1926. Janet Lewis was born in Chicago, daughter of the poet, teacher, and novelist Edwin Herbert Lewis, and was educated at the University of Chicago, where she was a member of the Poetry Club. Before her move to the Southwest, she had worked at the American Consulate in Paris and, in Chicago, as a proofreader for *Redbook* and as a teacher. In 1928 the Winters left Santa Fe for Palo Alto, California, where Professor Winters joined the faculty of Stanford University. In California their son and daughter were born. Many of Lewis' works (poetry and prose) were issued by the West's foremost poetry publisher, Alan Swallow, of Denver. In the early 1950's, Janet Lewis received a Guggenheim Fellowship.

I.    *The Ancient Ones*. Portola Valley, California: No Dead Lines, 1979.
      *The Earth-Bound*. Aurora, New York: The Wells College Press,
      1946.
      *The Indians in the Woods*. 1922; rpt. Palo Alto, California: Matrix
      Press, 1980.
      *Poems, 1924-1944*. Denver: Alan Swallow, 1950.
      *Poems Old and New, 1918-1978*. Chicago and Athens: Swallow
      and Ohio University Presses, 1981.
II.   Crow, Charles L. *Janet Lewis*. Western Writers Series, No. 41.
      Boise, Idaho: Boise State University, 1980.
      Winters, Yvor. *Forms of Discovery*. Chicago: A. Swallow, 1967.


**Peggy Pond Church** (b. 1903-)

Peggy—officially, Margaret—Pond Church is a native Westerner, born
near what is now known as Valmora in northern New Mexico, and her
Western roots go farther back: O. A. Hadley, her mother's grandfather,
came to New Mexico in 1880; Ashley Pond, her father, came in 1898, and
founded the Los Alamos Ranch School. Peggy's education, however,
occurred in various sections of the country. She attended high schools in
Santa Fe, New Mexico, Norwalk, Connecticut, and Los Angeles, California and went on to Smith College in Massachusetts. She left Smith in 1924
to marry Fermor S. Church, who had come out from Connecticut in 1921
to teach at the Los Alamos Ranch School. Their three sons were born in
New Mexico in 1926, 1928, and 1932. Peggy Pond Church has published
five volumes of poetry and her verse has been included in the annual Borestone Mountain anthology; she has also published a prose memoir of Edith
Warner, *The House at Otowi Bridge*. Today, the poet lives in Santa Fe
where, in addition to her writing (she is presently working on a biographical
memoir of Mary Austin), she enjoys walking in the nearby mountains with
her dog, Baba-the-Turk.


I.    *Familiar Journey*. Santa Fe: Writers' Editions, 1936.
      *Foretaste*. Santa Fe: Writers' Editions, 1933.
      *New & Selected Poems*. Boise: Ahsahta Press, 1976.
      *The Ripened Fields: 15 Sonnets of a Marriage*. 1954; rev. ed.
      Santa Fe: Lightning Tree Press, 1978.
      *A Rustle of Angels*. Denver: Peartree Press, 1981.
      *Ultimatum for Man*. [Palo Alto, California,] Stanford University:
      James Ladd Delkin, 1946.

**Nellie Burget Miller** (b. 1875-d. 1952)

A native of Iowa and a graduate of Upper Iowa University in 1894, Mrs. Miller was 46 years old, the wife of a practicing physician, and the mother of two sons and one daughter when she was named the second poet laureate of Colorado in 1923. Miller had arrived with her husband in Colorado Springs in 1908, and during her 44 years in the city published a number of plays, composed a devotional study, edited an anthology of poetry for servicemen in WWII, and wrote three volumes of poetry. The Western publisher, critic, and poet Alan Swallow, whose Swallow Press issued her collected poems in 1947, declares in his essay, "Poetry of the West," that: "Nellie Burget Miller must be considered a poet of small but real accomplishment. She was for some time [29 years] poet laureate of Colorado and the only state poet laureate I ever heard of who acquitted herself worthily."

I. *In Earthen Bowls*. New York: D. Appleton and Co., 1924.
  *Pictures from the Plains and Other Poems*. New York: The Poets Press, 1936.
  *The Sun Drops Red*. Denver: Sage Books, 1947.

**Peggy Simson Curry** (b. 1911-)

Peggy Simson Curry has published poetry, fiction, and articles in a wide range of national magazines. She is an anthologist as well as the author of three adult novels, one juvenile novel, a text for writers, and a book of poetry which has gone through numerous editions and recently (1977) was revised, enlarged, and published by the Spirit Mound Press of South Dakota. Peggy Simson was born in 1911 in Scotland, but came to the West and received her B.A. degree from the University of Wyoming in 1936. In 1937 she married William Seeright Curry, by whom she had one son. Her husband has been Chairman of the English Department at Casper College in Wyoming where Mrs. Curry presently teaches creative writing. Since 1970 she has served as poet-in-residence for poetry programs in Wyoming and continues her teaching duties at Casper College.

I. *Red Wind of Wyoming*. 3rd ed. Denver: Sage Books, 1955.
  *Red Wind of Wyoming*. 3rd, rev. ed. Vermillion, South Dakota: Spirit Mound Press, 1977.

*Ann Stanford*

*Ann Stanford was born in Southern California and has spent most of her life there. She attended Stanford University, where she studied with the poet Yvor Winters. Her first poems were published in his anthology* **Twelve Poets of the Pacific** *and in* **The New Mexico Quarterly Review,** *whose poetry editor was Alan Swallow. Swallow published her first two volumes of verse. Since then her poetry and criticism has appeared in numerous journals and in several of Borestone Mountain Awards'* **Best Poems**. *From 1957 to 1967 she was a poetry reviewer for the Los Angeles* **Times** *and in 1957 began gathering material for her anthology* **The Women Poets in English**. *In 1962 she received a Ph.D. in American Literature from the University of California, Los Angeles, and joined the faculty of California State University, Northridge, where she currently teaches. She married the architect Ronald A. White in 1942. They have four children.*

# Ahsahta Press
## POETRY OF THE WEST

*MODERN-*

Norman Macleod, *Selected Poems*
Gwendolen Haste, *Selected Poems*
Peggy Pond Church, *New & Selected Poems*
Haniel Long, *My Seasons*
H. L. Davis, *Selected Poems*
Hildegarde Flanner, *The Hearkening Eye*
Genevieve Taggard, *To the Natural World*
Hazel Hall, *Selected Poems*
*Women Poets of the West: An Anthology*

*CONTEMPORARY-*

Marnie Walsh, *A Taste of the Knife*
Robert Krieger, *Headlands, Rising*
Richard Blessing, *Winter Constellations*
Carolyne Wright, *Stealing the Children*
Charley John Greasybear, *Songs*
Conger Beasley, Jr., *Over DeSoto's Bones*
Susan Strayer Deal, *No Moving Parts*
Gretel Ehrlich, *To Touch the Water*
Leo Romero, *Agua Negra*
David Baker, *Laws of the Land*
Richard Speakes, *Hannah's Travel*

BOISE STATE UNIVERSITY
BOISE, IDAHO 83725